Along
for the
Ride

MASCOT
B O O K S

www.mascotbooks.com

Along for the Ride: Living My Fantasies as a Flight
Attendant's Husband

I have tried to recreate events, locales, and conversations from my
memories of them. In order to maintain their anonymity in some
instances I have changed the names of individuals and places. I may
have changed some identifying characteristics and details such as
physical properties, occupations, and places of residence.

For more information, please contact:
Mascot Books
620 Herndon Parkway, Suite 320
Herndon, VA 20170
info@mascotbooks.com

Library of Congress Control Number: 2021910958

CPSIA Code: PRFRE0721A
ISBN-13: 978-1-64543-707-9

Printed in Canada

To my wife, children, and mom for always believing and supporting me in this endeavor. Without your strength, patience, and blessing, this book would have never gotten off the ground. I love you all!

Along for the Ride

Living My Fantasies as a Flight Attendant's Husband

C. J. Nicholas

Prologue

THIS BOOK CAME ABOUT FROM fourteen years of traveling on a buddy pass with my wife's airline and the true stories that we would tell our friends and colleagues when we came back home. Since most of these stories concluded with laughter, friends would usually say, "You guys should write a book." Well, after fourteen years of material, it was time. The names of the airline and people we encountered over fourteen years have been changed to protect the guilty, including my name and my wife's, so we don't get sued and fired from that said airline.

My wife, let's call her Alejandra, has been a flight attendant for over twenty years for a major airline that we will call Global Airlines, and I (C. J.) was put on her buddy passes in 2007 when we were still dating. Never in my wildest dreams could I have imagined what I would learn, endure, laugh at, and love about these trips. To say the least, they were never boring. I hope you enjoy these stories as much as we did telling them over the years.

1

Flying Standby

WHEN I TELL THEM THAT I fly for free, most people think it's fantastic and that my wife, family, and I are so lucky for seeing the world. Yes, you are correct: it is fantastic and we are lucky. But there are downsides as well, such as being stuck in an airport for days with three kids under the age of six and running out of diapers for the newborn because we should have left Wednesday and it's now Saturday, but because of the weather, air traffic, and everybody on the planet going to the same place we are, the chances of us leaving on the next flight from Dallas to El Paso are slim to none—and Slim left town. Therefore then deciding to drive twelve hours in a rented car with three exhausted, screaming children. (If you have the option to wait or to drive across the great state of Texas as I have done three times, choose waiting. I promise you'll still have some sanity left by the end of the trip.)

But the perks are pretty damn good—free flights, sometimes first class, and if you haven't been in first class, it is all that you have ever heard about and more: free drinks, sundaes, entertainment, reclinable seats (big perk), hot towel, amenity kit—it's fantastic. You're treated like royalty.

I would love to tell you that we get first class all the time, but the truth is that a normal trip to anywhere works for us. Let's say we are going to El Paso, Texas, where my wife's family is from. We look at flights a month out. We can see how many seats are available on my wife's work website for personal travel. Obviously, a month out, everything is wide open, and we are definitely getting seats in first class. Two weeks later, the flight is filling up. No chance at first class, but we should get on. A week later, the flight is full, and we're looking at new destinations or multiple stops to reach our destination. The day before the trip, we have two flights we can choose from, and we're going to need help from the non-rev gods to get on either of them. The day of the trip, wake up at 4 a.m., check flights for passenger list, number of seats, number of standby passengers, and year of seniority.

Standby works like this: once you list yourself for it, you go in order of seniority. For example, Alejandra is a 1996 hire, so she and any member of her family traveling with her would go before a 2001 hire—unless they have the trump card, *a vacation pass!* Then that 2001 hire would go before Alejandra. It's like holding four aces in poker: yes, someone may beat you with a straight or royal flush, but it's unlikely. Apparently, the airline hands out these vacation passes like manhole covers, and they are hoarded by every person who works for the airline. Think *Charlie and the Chocolate Factory* with the Golden Ticket or *John Wick* with the Gold Coins, either movie works for this reference. In our fourteen years of traveling, we've used maybe two vacation passes, and when we did, it was like we found out we were going to be punished by the airline gods for using these trump cards to travel.

Back to 4 a.m. and checking flights; if both are oversold, we go back to bed and try again tomorrow. If seats are available, we go. Over the years, since our family has grown to five, it's harder to get on than it was when it was just the two of us. I load the car with luggage and drive; Alejandra works the Global Airlines iPhone and lists us for two flights. The conversation to the airport is usually something like this: ·

"Chris, can you drive faster? We won't make it at your current speed," Alejandra says.

"Yes, love," I say and accelerate over seventy miles per hour on Route 20, which is a dimly lit, snaking road to the Newark Flight Crew Parking Lot.

"Ok, Houston is oversold. Looks like we are going to Denver. There're two seats, and we are number three on the list."

"Who is in front of us?" I ask.

"One positive space, and a 1994 hire."

"Why don't you put us on a vacation pass?" I say. (Big mistake. I should just nod my head.)

"Are you nuts?! Do you know how many I have? Like, three, and it's February, and we may need them for the rest of the year. I can't believe you would suggest that!"

This all happens as I'm breaking land and speed records to get to the Flight Crew Parking lot.

Once you leave Route 20, you enter a side street that has two other flight crew parking lots on both sides named after destinations, like Paris and Rome. The one we are going to is farther down the dead-end side street named "Cleveland" and guarded with a card keypad, followed by a railroad crossing-gate arm and retractable tire spikes that go away once the card keypad has been read and the red light turns green.

Once in the parking lot, you must find parking on a hill.

Don't park in the valley, because if you do, the chances of getting water damage inside your car increase by a factor of ten, because why should a drainage system work properly in Newark, New Jersey? After you park and unload the car, you walk (or run, depending on time) to the party bus depot, where you hurry up and wait for the party bus (think prom or bachelor/bachelorette party: you and fifty of your closest friends riding to the airport). These buses come every ten minutes in the summer. During the winter, not so much.

As the bus arrives, you wait as other airline personnel get off the bus to go first before you go on. This is like letting the pedestrians go in front of your car at the crosswalk; they have the right of way. Then you quickly load your luggage, find a seat, and pray this guy drives faster than ten miles per hour as he makes a stop at every party bus depot in the lot (conservatively, about twenty stops).

Congratulations, you have finally arrived at the airport. You now have a 750-foot walk to baggage claim and check-in. Since it's winter, there's usually ice, snow, and wind whipping at forty miles per hour. Oh, by the way, you have forty-five minutes to make your gate and get through security. No problem. Alejandra checks us in, and I drop the luggage off at the outside baggage claim. We then run to security, show my passport and her airline ID, and then walk slowly and methodically through the line for twenty minutes to get to the airport security guy. He looks at our IDs and waves us through. Now the stripping begins: shoes, belts, computers out of backpacks. Raise your hands, get scanned, redress quickly, find the Departures Board, and bust your ass to your gate.

I should preface that my wife is always late to everything except the airport, where she transforms into Olympic Gold Medalist Sprinter Jackie Joyner-Kersee as we run for our gate. She gets a text saying they are about to call standby names.

When we reach the gate, Alejandra goes to the gate agent, usually a nice person but sometimes a jerk depending on the day. It's early, so hopefully he is in a good mood. His name plate reads "Rob." Alejandra asks, "Did you clear standbys yet?"

"Not yet," Rob says in a stern voice. He reaches for the phone/microphone and says, "Mr. and Mrs. Janokowski, you have five minutes to come to the gate, or your seats will be given to someone else."

That someone else is us.

Now we play the waiting game, or what I like to call "Pray they don't make the flight." I don't wish any evil on Mr. and Mrs. Janokowski. I'm sure they are very good people. I am just hoping they overslept, or got stuck in traffic, or had crazy-exhausting, all-night sex and can't get out of bed.

Two minutes left, Alejandra says, "We need to make this flight; the rest of the day is oversold."

"Great," I say sarcastically.

One minute left.

Alejandra and I say a prayer that the Janokowskis miss the deadline.

"Mr. and Mrs. Nicholas?" Rob yells.

"Right here," we say. We show our IDs, get our boarding passes, scan them, and scurry to our seats.

Alejandra is in 37B, and I am in 39E (both middle seats in separate rows, but we are on the flight to Denver).

But we are not out of the woods yet. Only when the door is closed can we know that we've officially made it. They can pull standbys off a flight if the paying passengers arrive in time. Now we play the game "Close the Fucking Door!"

Five more minutes pass, and Alejandra and I are anxiously

hoping we're not pulled off.

Then we hear an angel's voice: the lead flight attendant who says, "Ladies and gentlemen, we have closed the door. All large electronics need to be turned off and stowed. Please, power down your cell phones or put them on airplane mode."

We made it. Alejandra and I look at each other, nod, and mouth, "Love you."

The glamour, the rush, the nervousness—just a typical, normal day when you fly standby!

2

San Juan, Puerto Rico

MY FIRST TRIP WITH ALEJANDRA, then my girlfriend, happened in February 2007. We had been dating for about six months when Alejandra put me on her buddy passes. When we first started dating, Alejandra asked me, "Do you like to travel?"

"Absolutely, I love to travel," was my response, which apparently was the right answer since I was dating this smoking hot flight attendant.

Our first trip together started out like this on a Wednesday in February: "I can pick up a two-day San Juan turn this weekend, and the flight is wide open [meaning, you can get on the flight]. What do you think?" Alejandra asked.

"Where will we stay? Do I need to rent a hotel room?" I asked.

"No, Global Airlines puts us up in the hotel for free, and you stay with me," Alejandra stated cheerfully.

"So, let me get this straight: I fly for free, stay for free, go to the beach for the weekend, and fly back for free?"

"Yep," said Alejandra.

"And you'll be my personal flight attendant?"

"If you get first class," she stated in a sultry voice and gave me a seductive look.

After thinking for literally point-two seconds about seeing my girlfriend in her flight attendant uniform and in a bikini for the weekend in San Juan (insert two-day porn role-playing fantasy here), where the weather is eighty-five degrees in February compared to ten in New Jersey, I stated nonchalantly, "I'm in."

I should describe Alejandra to you. She is thirty-four years old, Latina, average height, 120 pounds, has long jet-black hair, brown skin, brown almond eyes, a smile that lights up a room, an athletic figure, and an infectious personality. (For the guys, she is the hottest thing under the sun, has an incredible ass and drop-dead gorgeous, long legs, and was the best sex I have ever had).

I am thirty-six, with short, cropped brown hair, six feet, 180 pounds, rugged (think Daniel Craig from James Bond), athletic, happy-go-lucky, and falling madly in love more and more with Alejandra every day.

We would leave after work on Friday. Since we were both teachers, Alejandra flew part-time during this time period. (We met at work. Alejandra has her teaching degree from the University of Texas El Paso.) We drove to school that day. Alejandra had her flight attendant uniform in the car and the last period of the day off, so she could change in the women's faculty upstairs bathroom in the two story wing of James Madison Middle School.

During lunch, she said, "The flight is filling up. You are definitely not getting first class, but you'll get on the flight."

"Ok," I said, disappointed because I really wanted her as my personal flight attendant on the flight and had never been in first class before. Again, feeding the porn fantasy of her being the sexy flight attendant and I the disgruntled passenger with her there to cater to my every need. Oh well, perhaps another time, or at least in the hotel room. Definitely in the hotel room.

Alejandra packed for both of us the night before (side note: flight attendants are expert packers)—the usual beachwear, swimsuit, flip flops, sun block, T-shirt. There wasn't much to pack for a two-day trip. I brought a red Swissgear backpack for personal items, passport, phone, a book, and most importantly, condoms.

We arrived at Newark Airport. It was an 8 p.m. flight, so no rush to break land and speed records to get there. There was no luggage because all my stuff was in her roller board. We went through security without problems and headed to the elevators in Terminal 2, where the flight attendants checked in. I was not allowed to go with her, so I hung out by a newsstand until she came back up.

I saw her smiling face, and we walked over to our plane, which was in the middle of the three-sectioned Terminal 2. When we arrived, I met the other flight attendants, two males and a female. The lead flight attendant was over six feet, 175 pounds, about twenty-seven years old, a tall drink of Latino water, and a very nice guy we'll call Seth. The other male flight attendant was shorter, 190 pounds, about mid-thirties, muscular, Latino, nice, and here dubbed James. The other female flight attendant was tall, 130 pounds, late twenties, unnatural, blonde, shoulder-length hair, brown skin, Latina, nice breasts, and a good ass. (Not that I was looking, Alejandra. I mean, I'm happily married now, and we were dating at the time, and I'm just describing her in detail for the readers. There was no physical attraction at all. But if she'd wanted to stay with us for a night, I would have been totally cool with it.) Let's call her Maria.

Alejandra went to the gate agent and asked her, "How does the flight look? My boyfriend is on standby."

The gate agent (a chubby blond woman in her fifties named Barbara) said, "It doesn't look good; he might not get on."

I looked at Alejandra, terrified, and asked her, "So what happens if I don't get on the flight?"

"You take my keys and go back to the apartment. I still have to work the flight. Wait for me till early Sunday night," Alejandra said cheerfully.

Now I was about to freak out. "Let me get this straight: I stay in exotic New Jersey, and you go to San Juan for the weekend?"

"Yes," she said.

Seth overheard our conversation and said with a smile, "We'll get him on even if we have to stow him aboard."

This move was totally illegal and against airline policy and FAA regulations, and Seth and everyone else on the flight would have been fired on the spot if this were to happen, but luckily he was only joking about it. Alejandra and crew had to board as she gave me the keys to the car and the key card pass so I could get out of the employee lot to drive home. She also gave me a kiss and said, "I'll pray you get on."

I said, "Me too."

I watched her board and then played the game, "Please, paying passengers, don't make the flight."

The gate agent announced, "Welcome, ladies and gentlemen, to flight 559 to San Juan. We will now board first class, all military personnel, and any families traveling with children ages two or under."

Over the loudspeaker, the gate agent said, "Group 1, please board."

"Where are you on the standby list," Alejandra texted.

"Third," I replied.

"Groups 1 and 2 please board," the gate agent called.

Ten minutes passed. "Groups 1 through 5, please board flight 559 to San Juan."

"Sanderson?" said Barbara, the gate agent.

I texted Alejandra, "They are clearing non-revs."

"Miller?" the gate agent asked.

"Nicholas?"

"Right here." I gave Barbara my passport. She scanned my ticket, and I ran down the jetway. I walked on the plane and saw the most beautiful flight attendant in the world smiling at me excitedly.

"May I see your ticket, sir?" she said.

"Sure," I said, going along with the facade that I didn't know her.

"Ah, 7D, right after the curtain on the left," Alejandra said in her most professional voice.

"Thank you."

I sat in 7D, literally the row behind first class where Alejandra was working, or what I liked to think of as the separation of the first-class passengers from the people in steerage, the part that becomes an escape pod when the plane goes down. Everyone in first class survives like James Bond, while the rest of us in coach die in the Atlantic Ocean, eaten by this week's giant ocean beast. If only I'd paid more for first class—or paid at all, for that matter.

The door closed, and the flight attendants did their thing with the safety procedures. I tried to see Alejandra in first class, but Seth was in front of me and the bulkhead wall that separates first class from coach. After all the "I'm going to get on, not going to get on" jazz, I really needed a drink to settle my nerves. As if on cue, Seth arrived with the bar cart, "What would you like to drink, sir?" he asked.

"Vodka and 7-up, please," I said.

"We don't have 7-Up. Does Sprite work?"

"Yes."

Seth gave me a can of Sprite and two mini bottles of Skyy Vodka for free, then proceeded to the next customer. Seth became my second favorite flight attendant on that flight. I poured all the vodka from one mini-bottle in the ice-filled cup and added a splash of Sprite. I took a sip and said to myself, "Ah, that hits the spot."

During the flight, I read my book and drank my vodka. It was around 10:30 p.m. Most of the cabin was dark and the service completed. Alejandra waved for me to come up to first class next to her. I was skeptical, because I am a rule-follower to the letter, and breaking the rules was never my thing. They have that curtain up for a reason, right? So coach passengers can't infiltrate first class? Plus, the two bouncers hidden in first class will jump out of nowhere, probably from the overhead compartments, and take you to the ground and sound the alarm, "Intruder alert! Intruder alert!"

She gave me an insistent look and patted the seat next to her. I did as she said because she was my girlfriend and knew better. (Note to the men reading this book: women always know better; stop trying to fight it. I still fight it, though; I can't take my own advice sometimes. It's just the man in me.)

I went through the curtain into the first class cabin where everyone was passed out asleep and sat next to Alejandra on the jump seat. No bouncers, no alarm. Who knew? "Hi," I said to Alejandra.

"Hi. How's your flight going?" Alejandra gave my hand a squeeze.

"Fine. Seth hooked me up with free vodka."

"Nice. He's a good guy."

"He's my second favorite flight attendant on this flight," I said.

She laughed, and in walked Seth to the first class galley and said, "I have to come up here. I just walked in on Maria and James. They were going at it like a couple of teenagers in the back galley."

I was like, "What?! They are making out in the back?"

"Oh yes, honey," Seth said. "This is not uncommon."

Did he just call me "honey"?

Alejandra laughed and said, "It's true. This has happened before with other people."

I was thinking, *Man, did I pick the wrong fucking career*. How many straight male flight attendants were there in the entire fleet? Six? If I were a flight attendant, I'd be getting laid six ways from Sunday. What an idiot I was!

Why am I blaming myself? I should have blamed my high school guidance counselor for not guiding me in the direction. I mean, I graduated from an all-boys high school. You'd think they would say something like, "Chris, after being sexually repressed in an all-boys high school for four years, go get laid in college, then go become a flight attendant. You'll have more sex than a porn star, and you'll get paid for it."

I would have run to the airlines for a flight attendant position. They could've hired and paid me in sand, and I would have accepted the job. I mean, that's the guidance young people should be getting, but I digress. That idea is for a different book.

I was still in shock that this stuff was happening in the back of the plane. With an hour left in the plane ride, Maria came up front looking a little disheveled but oddly satisfied. Coincidence or psychic phenomenon? She headed to the galley on the left side of the plane, straightened her uniform, took out her red lipstick and small mirror. She looked in the mirror, and said, "I need to put on my landing lips."

Apparently, her lipstick got messed up during the flight, or it got messed up on James' lips or other parts of his anatomy. Either way, I was laughing, and she gave a little wink to Alejandra and me.

Alejandra told me, "You need to go back to your seat. We're starting our descent. Let everyone get off the plane, and then we'll walk off together."

"Okay, love," I said and headed back to my seat, thinking about what the average passenger doesn't see behind the curtain and laughing to myself.

We landed, and I waited for all the passengers to leave. I was the last to leave and walked with the crew through the jetway. I was introduced to the Captain and first officer as we walked through San Juan Airport. Alejandra introduced me as her fiancé, which was a little shocking, but she told me that she had to say so; otherwise, I'd be taking a cab to the hotel. Captain Ron and First Officer Brian were cool with me riding in the crew shuttle.

During the shuttle ride, I kept my mouth shut because I didn't want to get Alejandra in trouble. And I was a little tired. We got to the hotel and received our key cards from the front desk. Our room was on the fifth floor of the hotel and had glass see-through elevators so we could look down and see the restaurant below, which was surprisingly full for midnight.

We put the key card into the slot, and I walked in first to check it out and make sure we weren't surprised by anyone. Once I gave Alejandra the all-clear sign, she came in, and we embraced and kissed passionately. "We need to shower. We have all the airplane gunk on us," she said.

"Anything I can do to help the environment," I joked.

We got undressed and entered the shower, where I did a

thorough job of cleaning Alejandra, especially her breasts, ass, and pussy, because I run a full-service operation when it comes to cleaning beautiful women, and I don't want my reputation tarnished with a bad review. She was happy with the job and expressed her opinion loudly and passionately.

"That was fantastic," she said.

"Thank you. I was really on my game tonight," I said. "I'm going to put it on social media, if you don't mind."

She laughed and called me a jerk, and we left the shower, dried off, and went to bed.

The next morning, Alejandra and I played a little more one-on-one in bed, and then dressed for the beach. She wore a blue bikini, a multi-colored wrap around her waist, a straw sunhat, sunglasses, and flip flops. I wore a dark blue bathing suit, white Nike T-shirt and visor, and flip flops.

We had breakfast at the hotel restaurant and saw Captain Ron and First Officer Brian eating together. We went over and said hello. They had the same idea we did, as they were dressed in beachwear as well.

"What do you think, babe?" asked Alejandra as we sat down to eat.

"This is amazing. I can't believe we're here. Thank you for taking me," I said.

We made small talk and finished our breakfast.

The beach was a three-block walk straight from the hotel. We paid to enter it, along with the entry fee and chairs. We enjoyed our beach day, soaking up the sun and sand and water, which was as calm as a lake and seventy degrees. The beach was fantastic: golden sand, light blue sea. One word: *paradise*. We spent five hours on the beach and headed back to the hotel to shower up, to then head back to Newark on that night's flight.

On the way out, we saw Maria sitting alone in a red bikini on her beach chair. We said hi and asked if she'd seen anyone else from the crew.

"James just left," she said. "He's tired. He had a long night last night." Maria smiled and winked at us.

My jaw dropped, and Alejandra said, "Goodbye," as we walked back to our hotel.

On the way, Alejandra asked me, "What are you thinking about?"

"I'm thinking that I chose the wrong career path in life."

She shoved me. "C'mon, you horn dog. Let's go back to the room."

3

Paris to Rome to London to Madrid to Amsterdam to Ocean Beach, New Jersey

AS I STATED BEFORE, ALEJANDRA and I met as teachers at James Madison Middle School, becoming friends first and later boyfriend and girlfriend. It was Memorial Day weekend, and I was working in my school district. If the school district doesn't use all its allotted snow days, then they get used in the late spring/early summer. These are called "Snow Give Back Days," and whoever came up with this genius invention should receive the Nobel Peace Prize. Extra days off to golf, go to the beach, or go on vacation. It's a sweet perk of being an educator.

In the academic school year of 2006–07, New Jersey had a very mild winter. We'd used only two snow days, in March of all months, so we got three "Snow Give Back Days." In April, the "Snow Give Back Days" were announced after the board meeting, and when they're announced, it's like the E. F. Hutton's tagline:

"When E. F. Hutton talks, people listen." Teachers' phones blow up with texts about golf, vacation, and getting together. This year, two of the days would bracket Memorial Day weekend, meaning we would be off on the Friday before Memorial Day and the Tuesday after. Five whole days off in late May! The other "Snow Give Back Day" was the first Friday of June for a three-day weekend.

Alejandra read the news via email about the "Snow Give Back Days" and immediately texted me: "Do you want to go to Europe for the five-day weekend?"

I replied, "Fuck yeah!"

"Let's look at flights tonight."

"Okay."

Later that evening in our Victorian brownstone apartment in Jersey City, New Jersey, located in "The Heights" section of Jersey City bordering Hoboken, Alejandra was sitting on her orange easy chair in a white T-shirt and pink checkered shorts, looking at flights to Europe on the laptop. I was in the enormous kitchen pouring myself an Arizona ginseng iced tea from the gallon jug in the refrigerator.

"Babe, the flights are wide open," Alejandra yelled from the living room.

"Great, where?" I asked.

"Everywhere in Europe. Where do you want to go?"

"Rome."

"I was thinking Paris," Alejandra said.

"Okay, that works, too. I'm easy," I said.

She laughed. "Don't I know it."

I smiled.

Three days out, flights were still wide open to Paris, and we even might get first class. We started researching hotels and places to stay in Paris. We didn't need a five-star hotel, only a bed to sleep and do what by now you know we do. I don't need to repeat myself, but I will if you want me to. Just wait for the kinky sex we have in Paris, or continue reading. (FYI, this isn't a choose-your-own adventure book). We booked a two-star hotel near the metro in a decent neighborhood of Paris.

The day of our trip, Thursday, May 24, we woke up, and the flights were wide open. We listed for first class, knowing that we'd get it. We packed and left for work. Unfortunately, we couldn't leave until after 3 p.m., because it was a "black-out day." Black-out days are days before and after a vacation that you can't be absent for, or you will get docked. So, in this scenario, the black-out days were Thursday, May 24, and Wednesday, May 29. And whoever created this fucking "black-out day" system is a complete fucking asshole.

Since it was May and the school year was almost over, the Parent Association had thrown the faculty a "Teacher Appreciation Breakfast" in the cafeteria that morning. It consisted of bagels, cream cheese, butter, an assorted fruit bowl, coffee, tea, and crumb cake. Basically carb heaven, or if you are one of those gluten-free people, your hell. We got in line, me in a striped light-blue Polo shirt and khaki pants, Alejandra in a white blouse and light blue dress. She looked amazing as always. I picked a cinnamon raisin bagel with cream cheese and a coffee; she got fruit and coffee. We thanked the parents and sat in the cafeteria at a table with our mutual friends.

"What are you guys doing for the break?" Joe asked.

Alejandra answered, "We're going to Paris."

"Nice, when?" Joe said.

"Right after school, the 6:30 p.m. flight."

Joe and I shared a wink and a nod of approval (this is the

"unspoken man language," you're-going-to-get-laid-multiple-times-by-a-beautiful-woman-in-a-foreign-country look).

During the school day, the weather was hot and humid. Around 12:30 p.m., the heavens opened up and a deluge came down, thunder and lightning, Biblical stuff happening. Alejandra texted me: "Flights are still open. Don't delay after school. Lock your classroom and meet me in the parking lot."

I replied, "Will do."

When the bell rang, it was a mad rush to get to the parking lot, between the sea of middle school students trying to walk home and the teachers rushing to start their vacation. I arrived at Alejandra's black Hyundai, where she was waiting for me. I got in the passenger's seat, and we were off to the airport.

Alejandra is a very good driver. Her father, Raul, was a Hall of Fame dirt track racecar driver in Ciudad Juarez, Mexico, and taught her to drive. This experience has apparently anointed her as a Hall of Fame racecar driver as well (according to her). As always, we were breaking land and speed records to get to Newark Airport to the flight crew parking lot. Alejandra was not working the flight, but we could still park there. We parked, waited for the bus, got on the bus after the other flight attendants and pilots got off (again, they had the right of way), and headed to the airport. We got through security and headed to the middle section of Terminal 2. Alejandra got on her computer and checked the flights. "Paris is at negative twenty," she said.

"What!" I said. "How?"

"I don't know. It was wide open when we left and when I checked it during ninth period. I'm going to ask the gate agent."

A couple minutes later, Alejandra came back.

"What's up?" I asked.

"We're not going to Paris. Newark Airport was shut down

because of the storm, so a lot of people missed their flights and are now trying to make their connections, bumping us off our flight," she said.

"That sucks. Now what?"

"Why not Rome? The gate is right next to Paris. Let me check the flights."

Alejandra is one of the most positive people I know, which is probably one of the reasons I am so attracted to her—besides her incredible body and the amazing sex. Let me put that in a better order for you: amazing sex, incredible body, and a really positive person.

"Rome is open. It leaves at 7 p.m. I'm listing us," she said.

"Don't we need to get a hotel?" I asked.

"We will get one when we arrive," she said.

At 6:30 p.m., Paris had left without us, and we were now in danger of getting bumped off Rome as well.

"Rome is now oversold by ten," Alejandra said.

"Fuck."

Alejandra looked around at the other gates. "London?"

"Sure, and I know the language, which helps," I joked.

"It's open. I'm listing us."

"What time is the flight?" I asked.

"7:30 p.m.," she said.

Rome had now left, so we were watching London closely. "It's oversold by fifteen," she said.

"Fuck me," I said angrily. "What else is there?"

"Madrid is open. Leaves at eight?"

"List us," I said.

It was 7:30 p.m. London was gone, and now the computer said that Madrid was oversold by eighteen.

Alejandra went to the gate agent by the Amsterdam flight,

whom she happened to be friends with (let's call her Tammy), and asked, "Is there any chance we can get on the 9 p.m. flight?"

Tammy shook her head. "Go home. You guys aren't getting on anything tonight because of the storm."

Alejandra and I were flabbergasted. We had spent the past five hours trying to get to Europe with no luck whatsoever.

We headed home to our apartment, showered and looked at flights for the following day.

"Everything is oversold, Europe and domestic," Alejandra said, frustrated. "We have a five-day weekend, and we are stuck in Jersey City."

"I have an idea," I said. "My mom has a beach house in Ocean Beach, New Jersey. We can go there and hang out on the beach for the next four days."

"Why not?" Alejandra said. "Let's go to the beach."

We woke up the next day and drove an hour and a half to Ocean Beach, New Jersey, to meet my mom at her two-bedroom shore house. The next four days were filled with sun and fun at the beach. Life lesson: When life gives you lemons, make lemonade.

4

Paris for Real

ON MY THIRTY-SIXTH BIRTHDAY, ALEJANDRA surprised me with one of the greatest presents I have ever received: the gift of experience. We sort of made a rule in the fourteen years we've been together: we would rather give experiences than items as gifts. My birthday is December 6, and like all December birthday people, I get screwed because of the holidays. Gifts are usually smaller in amount than, say, a June birthday. It was on a Thursday in 2007, and I was reading the note that Alejandra had written in my birthday card: "We are going to Paris this weekend."

"You're kidding," I said disbelievingly.

"No. Tomorrow night, 7 p.m. flight. It's wide open, and we are listed for first class and should get it," she said cheerfully. "Oh, and this is going to be a three-day weekend, so we are calling out sick on Monday."

I jumped up and kissed her. "Thank you. I love you," and totally forget about the gift lying at my feet.

"Aren't you going to open up your present?" she asked.

"There's more? I thought that was the gift," I said. I opened the gift bag, and inside were size 12, beautiful, brown leather loafers. "They're beautiful, thank you."

"You can wear them this weekend to break them in," Alejandra said.

"I will."

Now, I'm always a planner, but Alejandra is very spontaneous. We are sort of the yin and yang to each other. Ten minutes after receiving the gift, I asked Alejandra a bunch of questions: "Don't we need a hotel? How are we getting to the hotel? Do we need a plan for getting to all the sights we're looking to see?"

"Relax. We'll get a hotel tonight, and we'll figure everything else out in Paris," Alejandra said.

Alejandra booked a two-star hotel and informed me that we didn't need much because we were there to sleep and shower, then hit the ground running.

The next day, we went to work and told no one where we were going that weekend because (1) we are calling out "cough, cough," sick on Monday, and the fewer people who knew about it, the better, and (2) we obviously upset the non-rev gods in May, so loose lips sink ships.

The day was a normal day, if there ever is one as a teacher. The bell rang to end the school day, and Alejandra and I were back in the black Hyundai on our way to Newark Airport, breaking land and speed records along the way.

We got to the airport and through security, no problem. Alejandra checked her company phone, and bingo!: we had first class tickets to Paris. Call me "Mr. Papagiorgio" (from *Vegas Vacation*), sitting in high society. This was the first time I had ever been in first class and the first time I'd ever been to Europe, crossing the Atlantic Ocean.

I should preface that I'm deathly afraid of sharks, ever since I saw the original *Jaws* on HBO when I was a nine-year-old kid. It's so bad that when I go in the ocean, I make sure that there is at least one person in front of me, behind me, to the left, and to the right of me. This way, if the shark wants me, he's got to earn it.

So we got to our seats in first class, and we received our amenity kit, the hot towel, and free drinks. Not bad, this is traveling, baby!

Alejandra saw the shit-eating grin on my face and said, "What do you think?"

"Can we travel like this all the time?"

She laughed. "Happy birthday, Mr. Papagiorgio." She kissed me on the lips. "Listen, when we get to Paris, we're not allowed to check in 'til 3 p.m. their time, so get some sleep on the flight after dinner. We are going to hit the ground running once we get there. We'll sleep at 3 p.m. in our hotel."

Dinner came, and it was fantastic. I had steak, and Alejandra had a chicken dish. The sundae was perfect. I was watching the *Bourne Identity* on the screen, and things were good.

Alejandra put on her sleeping mask and reclined her seat. "Babe, you should go to sleep."

"I can't," I told her.

"Why?"

"Well, I'm deathly afraid of sharks, and right now we're currently seven miles up over the Atlantic Ocean. I'm sorry, but that's what's running through my head right now," I confess.

"Chris, this fear of yours is totally irrational," she said.

"How so?"

"First of all, if anything happens to the plane, you won't have any oxygen and will suffocate because the air is so thin. Second, when you hit the ocean water at 700 mph, it's like hitting concrete. The plane will explode. There's no chance for survival. Good night," she said cheerfully, and she put her sleeping mask over her eyes and went to sleep.

"Well, thanks, Stephen King, that was the worst bedtime story I have ever heard," I replied.

Now I was thinking about shoulder rolling at 700 mph and crashing into the ocean. Thanks, Alejandra. I called the flight attendant over and asked her for another Skyy vodka and Sprite. I told her, "Even if my hand is down, it's really up for a refill."

The flight attendant laughed and said, "Okay."

So after a couple of drinks and three movies, I finally relaxed and fell asleep. Half an hour later, we landed at Charles de Gaulle Airport in Paris. I was exhausted, but Alejandra was bright-eyed and bushy-tailed and talking a mile a minute. "How was your sleep? What do you mean you didn't sleep at all? I told you to go to sleep!"

I should explain that I'm not a morning person. Never have been, never will be. Alejandra is a morning person, and it's hell. Non-stop questions. I'm like, let me drink my coffee in peace so I can become human again and, as Depeche Mode once sang, "Enjoy the Silence." It's a yin and a yang of a morning relationship.

We landed and took a train to our hotel. When you land in France, you're an hour outside of Paris by train. Our plan was to get to our two-star hotel in Paris, where hopefully they'd let us in early to shower, sleep, and then hit the town. But our first problem after we claimed our luggage was to find the train station from the airport. Alejandra did all the talking because she is bilingual in Spanish and English and took high school French, while I only kiss that way.

Rather than go to information (which is clearly marked *information*, but say it with a French accent so you can truly appreciate the moment), Alejandra walked right up to a French soldier armed with a submachine gun, who was on patrol, for directions. I followed behind her, thinking, "What would possess you to ask *him* for directions?"

She rushed back to me. "Okay, I got directions. Down the escalator and to the right," she said excitedly.

It was a rainy day in France as we bought our train tickets and waited for our ride. After ten minutes, we got on and found our seats. I looked out the window at the graffiti on the walls as we passed all the rural towns heading toward Paris. I put my head on Alejandra's shoulder and fell asleep.

She woke me up as we made our stop. I let out a big yawn, and we got off the train with our roller-board luggage. It was another ten-minute walk to our hotel, and it hadn't stopped raining. It was cold and raw outside. I put on my black wool New York Yankee hat and black leather gloves. Nothing screams, "Hey, I'm an American," like a New York Yankee hat.

When we reached the hotel, I was exhausted and hoping that the travel gods would take mercy on my soul and let us check in early and sleep. The concierge saw us and asked, in French, if he could help us.

Alejandra asked, "Is it possible for us to check in early?"

The concierge switched to English and said in his Jacque Custeau accent, "I'm sorry, madam, but we can't check you in until three p.m. We are fully booked, and checkout isn't until 11 a.m. and then we have to clean the rooms."

I looked at the clock: 10:30 a.m.

"Can we leave our luggage here while we see the town and come back by 3 p.m.?" Alejandra asked.

"Of course, madam." Jacque motioned for her to take our luggage and put it behind his counter.

"Okay, Chris, let's go," she said to me. We put our luggage behind the counter.

"We would like to go sight-seeing. Is there anything close to the hotel?" Alejandra asked Jacque.

"*Oui*, Madam. Notre Dame is two metro stops away." He pulled out a metro map and pointed to it.

Alejandra said to me, "Let's go."

"You trust that guy with our luggage?" I said as we walked to the metro.

"Stop, he's fine. Nothing is going to happen to our luggage," she said.

Ten minutes later, we got out of the metro, walked up the steps, and saw Notre Dame about 200 yards to our left. We walked past a bunch of gift shops on the way. As we were walking, we saw the round gold plates that were shown in *The Da Vinci Code*. They were about five inches in diameter and spaced out every ten feet.

I pointed them out to Alejandra, and she was like, "Cool."

We walked into Notre Dame, and it was magnificent. As Catholics, it was one of the most beautiful churches we had ever been to. We took pictures, but my patience was low because I was tired, and Alejandra was playing the role of photographer/ director, saying, "Do this . . . do that . . . now light a candle and look up." Needless to say, my face in those photos said, "Take the fucking picture already."

We finally left Notre Dame and headed to a cafe to get lunch and a cafe Americano so I could get some energy. My fuel cells were on "E." Since I couldn't read French, I had to play the "I'm the deaf-mute" game and point to what I wanted to eat. The only words I know in French are *oui* (yes), *merci* (thanks), *bonjour* (good morning), and *voulez vous coucher avec moi* (do you want to sleep with me tonight [from the Lady Marmalade song]). And really, that's all the French you need, in my book, except for maybe how to order alcoholic drinks. I ordered a meat dish. It was good, and my coffee helped me become human again.

"What do you think?" Alejandra asked.

"It's amazing, but I'm so tired."

"You should have slept on the plane," she reminded me.

"Yes, love."

After lunch, we walked around and saw the brown, murky Seine River, "Just like the Hudson," I said to Alejandra.

She laughed and said, "Shut up before they deport you."

We strolled along the Seine, took a bunch of pictures, and headed back to the hotel. On our walk back to the metro, we hit a couple of different gift shops, one called "Bonjour de Paris" where I came across a sex die, a wooden die about an inch high and wide, with six sides, but instead of dots, it had pictures of six different sexual positions that you and your partner could try.

Alejandra said, "I got a Christmas ornament for our Christmas tree."

"I got a sex die for our bedroom!"

She looked at me, then at the sex die, blushed, rolled her eyes, and shook her head.

In my defense, I was left unsupervised. We paid separately, because Alejandra was embarrassed that I was buying the sex die. But I told her, "You'll warm up to it once we start playing with it."

Again, she rolled her eyes.

C'mon. It was a little funny.

We got to our hotel and checked in, retrieved our luggage from around the counter, and headed to the one-person elevator with the bellhop. Since Alejandra and I couldn't fit together with our luggage (one bag per person) in the elevator, we went up one at a time. The bellhop said, "I'll meet you on the third floor."

Alejandra went first with her bag, and then I followed. There was literally no room with my bag and myself. I reached the third floor and found the bellhop and Alejandra outside the door, trying to get into our room. Apparently, the door was stuck. Our bellhop turned the key, threw his right shoulder, and, *voilá*, it opened.

"State-of-the-art security," I said.

The bellhop said, "It gets stuck from time to time."

"Riigghhtt," I retorted.

He handed me the key, showed us the room, and left. I locked the door, and we immediately headed for the shower to get the airplane gunk off. We got to the bathroom, but there was no shower curtain. What kind of country was this? Who doesn't have a shower curtain? It costs $1.75 at K-Mart in the States. They must have seen one on TV or in the movies.

"There's no shower curtain," I said to Alejandra.

"I see that," she said.

"How are we going to shower?" I asked.

"Well, there's a tub, and the shower has a portable head, so . . . carefully," she exclaimed.

We showered individually, yet there was water everywhere. We used more towels on the floor than on our own bodies. We hung the drenched towels over the tub hoping they would dry sometime by 2075. We got into our pajamas and went to bed. Alejandra set the alarm for 8 p.m. so we could get up, have dinner, and go to the Eiffel Tower.

My head hit the pillow, and I was out. The alarm went off, and the previous five hours felt like five minutes. We got up, changed clothes, and headed out "Hotel Sticky Door" to a restaurant. Alejandra likes to eat where the locals eat, so we found a restaurant near the hotel. It looked like a glass circus tent, and we walked into a smokehouse. Everyone smoked. In fact, there were two sections: smoking and ultra-smoking. We sat down and looked at the menus. Everything was in French (no English translation), but the menu had pictures, so I was okay. I pointed to a chicken dish and asked for a gas mask for the two of us. The waiter didn't understand my humor and gave me a confused look. So I just smiled and waved.

The food was good. We paid our bill, and I asked for a card so I could sue them for secondhand smoke disease in twenty years, but they didn't give me one. We headed to the metro to go see the Eiffel Tower. It was about a twenty-minute ride, and from the metro, it was another mile walk to the tower. It was raining hard once we exited the metro. Alejandra had an umbrella, a one-person umbrella, so trying to fit two people under it was an exercise in futility. But we tried it anyway. We exited the metro, and there it was, all lit up and beautiful. We walked the mile, and now my jeans were sticking to me. I was drenched, and my new shoes were killing me, biting at the top of my foot.

I told Alejandra.

"How are they hurting you?" Alejandra asked.

"They're biting the top of my foot," I said.

"Well, they look great, and looks are more important than comfort," she told me matter-of-factly.

"Who the hell told you that pile of bullshit? The most important purchases of your life are your bed and shoes because you're in them the most, and I buy both based on comfort. These shoes suck on comfort."

Alejandra gives me a look, saying, "Don't push your luck." So, I stayed quiet. I'd seen my girlfriend go full Latina, and God help you when she goes Ricky Ricardo machine-gun Spanish on you.

We arrived at the Eiffel Tower, and it was beautiful. We got in line and paid ten euros each to enter. I'm not a fan of heights, but I do love a good view if I look across and not down. That's the secret: Look down, you're screwed; across, you enjoy the view. We went up the elevator on one of the legs of the tower. Once we got in the middle of the tower, we took another elevator to the observation deck.

The observation deck is inside, thank God, and it's about thirty-feet wide and has a beautiful view overlooking Paris. Depending on what side you're on, you can see what country is in that direction. When you go to the east side of the deck, you see the United States of America 6,000 kilometers away (or something like that, because we're not on the metric system and I don't have the conversion chart in front of me).

Alejandra saw someone walking outside the deck and nudged me to go.

"Okay," I said.

We walked up a three-step metal staircase, opened the door, and, bam, we were outside. It was extremely narrow, about three-feet wide. The flooring was metal, and there was a railing. That's it. Oh, by the way, it was raining, windy, and the Eiffel Tower was shaking (they don't tell you this when you buy tickets at the booth). Plus, the soles of my shoes had no grip whatsoever. I thought, *This is it. This is how I go out.* We walked around, and Alejandra said, "This is amazing, isn't it?"

Remember when I said look across, not down? Yeah, I forgot to take my own advice, and I looked down. Now, I was gripping the railing with both hands and saying, "Sure is. Let's go back inside."

"Why?" Alejandra asked.

"Well, it's raining, windy, the Eiffel Tower is shaking, I have no grip in the soles of my shoes, and we are the only people crazy enough to be out here."

"Fine," she said, disappointed.

"Thank God," I said to myself.

We went back inside the observation deck and took the elevator down to safety and finally the ground. It was still pouring outside, and we had a mile walk to the metro. Alejandra and I started walking. Every thirty feet, she'd turn around and say, "Wow!"

After three times of that, I was like, "What are you doing?"

"I'm just admiring it," she said.

She did it three more times. It was still pouring rain, and we'd gone thirty feet in five minutes. I said, "Alejandra, if it moves, let me know. Otherwise, let's go. It's raining, and my feet are killing me."

"I'm just admiring it. What's your problem?" she said.

"My problem is that we have a mile walk ahead of us, my feet are killing me, I'm drenched to the bone, and it's taking us forever and a day to get to the metro station, because of every time you turn around."

"*Pinche guero*," she yelled.

This is her term of endearment for me. It means "fucking white boy."

We got on the metro and headed to "Hotel Sticky Door." We arrived at our room, and after turning the key, yep, you guessed it: the door was stuck. I tried the key again and threw my right shoulder into the door. It budged a little, but it was still stuck. Okay, a little more effort. I threw my shoulder into it fully this time, thinking I'd separated it now, and, boom, the door opened.

"State of the art," I said again.

Alejandra didn't respond. She was mad at me for yelling at her on the walk to the metro. She walked right by me.

I took my shoes and socks off, noticed the deep red marks on the top of my feet, and showed Alejandra. We then proceeded to take off our wet clothes, towel off, and get into pajamas. She was still mad.

I said, "I'm sorry I yelled at you. I was wrong."

She said, "I accept your apology."

We brushed our teeth and headed to bed.

In the review of "Hotel Sticky Door," it says that you are a block away from the metro station. It makes no mention that your room will shake every time a train pulls to a stop, so sleep comes and goes with the shaking throughout the night.

The next morning, it was sunny, and we got ready to head to the Louvre. We took the umbrella just in case and headed to a café for a cafe Americano and cappuccino and some *pain* (bread). We were sitting outdoors. It was about fifty degrees and sunny, but the clouds were moving very fast. Alejandra and I took out the metro map and found what line we would take to get there. After breakfast, we boarded the metro and headed to the Louvre. There was not a long line, but the weather was starting to turn for the worse. We got inside the Louvre, and, literally, the heavens opened up behind us.

We bought our tickets and started to walk around the Louvre. We saw the *Mona Lisa* and got the obligatory picture from fifty feet away because there is a wall and the *Mona Lisa* is guarded 24/7. We admired the paintings and statues, and we walked into a corridor full of naked male statues. Alejandra grabbed me, leaned into my ear, and whispered, "I'm getting really turned on here."

"Because of all the naked statues exposing themselves?" I replied.

"Yes," she said seductively.

"I can find us a bathroom?"

She laughed. "Tonight at the hotel. We can try out your sex die."

"Okay," I said, smiling.

(Note to self: take Alejandra to as many museums with naked male statues as humanly possible.)

We left the Louvre, got lunch at a café, headed toward the Arc de Triomphe and the Champs D'Elysee, and saw the shops Louis Vuitton, Yves St. Laurant, and Coach. It was the Fifth Avenue of Paris. After walking through the shops, I saw how much a purse was and decided right then and there to make sure Alejandra didn't drop 10,000 euros on a coin purse from Coach. Alejandra loves to shop; I do not. I would rather run face first into a brick wall at full speed, and continue to do so, than go shopping. But we were on the Champs D'Elysee, and when in Rome, or Paris for that matter, you do this.

After shopping, we headed to a café to people watch. It cost twenty euros for two cappuccinos.

Alejandra said, "You're paying for the view, not the drink."

"Actually, I think it's both that I'm paying for," I replied.

We sit, had our waiter take a couple of photos, and enjoyed our ten-euro drinks. We people watched and made small talk.

We headed back to the metro to go to a restaurant for dinner. We went to this place, about two blocks from our hotel, recommended by Jacque. He said it was very local, and he was right. It was a little hole-in-the-wall restaurant, dark, and surprisingly not smoky. We walked in, got a table for two, and had a crepe, because, hey, we were in Paris.

We recapped our day over dinner and talked about life. "This is amazing. Thank you for taking me again for my birthday," I said.

"No problem. We have a couple of places to hit tomorrow, and then we leave on Monday."

"Okay. Are you still horny from this afternoon?" I asked, hoping and praying the answer was yes.

"Yes." Alejandra smiled.

"How do you say *check* in French?"

She laughed.

We headed to "Hotel Sticky Door," got to the door, turned the key, threw the shoulder into it, and went in. We closed the door, locked it, and attacked each other. We started kissing hard as we undressed each other hungrily. I undid her top and bra. I cupped her breasts and tweaked her nipples. Alejandra let out a small moan. She grabbed my dick through my soaking wet jeans and started loosening my belt and unleashing my rock-hard cock.

"You liked seeing all those dicks in the Louvre?" I asked dominantly.

"Yes, it made me so wet," she said breathlessly.

I threw her on the bed and got my red Swissgear backpack, opened the front pocket where I kept the condoms, and grabbed one. I also grabbed the sex die.

"What did you bring with you?" Alejandra asked, seeing that there was more than just a condom in my hand.

"The sex die," I stated proudly. "Let's try it."

I rolled it on the bed. It showed a woman riding a man's face. "Looks like it's your lucky day," I said.

She laughed and clapped, but instead of her riding my face, I went down on her with Alejandra on her back. Truth be told, it's one of my favorite things to do to her. We proceeded to roll the sex die a couple of times that night.

Sunday morning, we woke up, got ready, and had breakfast at a small café, ordering the usual cafe Americano, cappuccino, and *pain*. It was sunny, and we headed to the Sacre Coeur, which is a basilica that has another incredible view of Paris because it takes 50,000 stairs to get up there. Once completing level fifty of our outdoor Stairmaster, we finally reached the Sacre Coeur, and there was a mass going on. So we celebrated the mass in French and then walked around afterward. From there, we walked back down the 50,000 stairs again and headed for lunch at a café near a park.

After lunch, we had to find a public phone to call out sick for the next day. These were the days before you could access the sick leave website via the internet. We had to physically dial a number, leave our name, school, grade we teach, and where our lesson plans were located so the substitute teacher could find them.

Alejandra asked the waiter in French, "Where is the nearest pay phone?"

He replied, "Down the road about a block away."

We walked there, and I went first. I dialed the number, left my name, school, grade I teach, and where my sub plans could be located. Alejandra got in the phone booth, punched in the number, and suddenly, from down the street, an ambulance and its siren were headed our way—you know, the European "whenah, whenah!" It was blasting at a rock concert decibel. It was so loud we couldn't even think.

To her credit, Alejandra was still giving her information over the phone. She came out.

"I may have to do that again," Alejandra said.

"What are you going to say, I'm sorry but there was a foreign ambulance passing by my house when I was calling out sick?"

"You're right. I hope they heard me, though," Alejandra exclaimed.

"I hope so too."

We had dinner, but Alejandra was worried and didn't say much over the meal. She normally talked a mile a minute.

"Do you want to try again to call out sick?" I asked.

"No, if I call out again, then they'll be suspicious."

"Okay, let the chips fall where they may. Thank you for a wonderful weekend—one that I will never forget."

"You're welcome. You're worth it," she said.

We flew back that Monday, coach this time, and got home to shower and sleep. Nothing exciting happened in coach, and we reported for work on Tuesday, hoping not to be called into the office first thing because of the French ambulance.

All day long, we sat on pins and needles. But there came no phone call from the principal, no reprimands. Nothing but broken-in, brown leather shoes.

5

Albuquerque, New Mexico to El Paso, Texas

IN THE 2000S, MY SCHOOL district's winter break would last a full week. Now it's two days. My superintendent used to call it "Energy Conservation Week" so that the public would understand why teachers and children had a full week off for no reason, but after a couple of years, the townspeople caught on. So now it's two days.

In 2007, Alejandra and I went to El Paso, Texas, to meet and visit her family. It is obviously a big step in any relationship to meet your girlfriend's parents, so I was excited and nervous.

There are no direct flights to El Paso from Newark, New Jersey, and the closest thing to direct is through Albuquerque, New Mexico, which is three and a half hours away by car. On Thursday, Alejandra looked at flights and saw that Saturday was our best bet for getting to El Paso because everything would be gone by the time we left work at 3 p.m. on Friday (black out day).

The flight left at 9 a.m. on Saturday, February 17, and there were seven seats available. Since this was a big trip, Alejandra used one of her Golden Ticket Vacation passes so we could get on. I was shocked and offered counseling.

"Are you okay with doing this? This is a big step for you. If you need some time to be alone, I will give it to you," I said in a pseudo-concerned voice.

"Oh, shut up, *pinche guero*," she said sarcastically.

I laughed, so did she, and we packed for the week: shorts, shirts, jeans, underwear, condoms—the usual items.

Friday came and went, and the flight was still at seven for standby passengers at 9 p.m. We decided to go to bed because we had to wake up at 6 a.m. and do the lightspeed trek to the airport.

At 6 a.m., Alejandra checked the flight. It was now at five available seats, and we were numbers four and five.

Alejandra said, "We may not get on, and the other flights are oversold. We can't check our bags. We are going to have to bring them to the gate, and then we will check them at the gate if we get on."

"Okay, let's hope we get on," I said.

We headed to the airport and went through security with our medium-size roller board luggage. Alejandra's is black with a hot pink bow on it so she can identify it when it comes out the luggage shoot, and mine is a blue one with a luggage tag in the shape of a football, for my identification purposes. We got through security and sprinted to the gate, which is in the middle of Terminal 2 all the way at the end and a floor below the main gate. It was 8:30 a.m.

When we descended the steps to the gate, we met a herd of people getting in line to board the plane. We checked the board to see the standby list and saw that we were still numbers four and five and that there were still five seats available. Alejandra checked the board and saw there was a person senior to her, but he used a personal pass, not a vacation pass. Therefore, he was number six.

As luck would have it, "number six" was standing right next to me and talking on the phone with someone, trying to get that person to change his reservation from personal to vacation pass via home computer. In 2007, you could not change your reservation via smartphone yet. So I was overhearing his conversation, which went like this: "Yes, go to Global Airlines Employee Travel. Then put in my username: O8462. Then my password: [he whispered it]. What do you mean it is not working?"

I told Alejandra, "I think that guy is number six, and he's trying to change his reservation."

"How do you know that?"

"I was eavesdropping on his conversation."

"Nice." She looked at her watch. "It's 8:45. It's too late for him to change it," she said happily.

"Nice," I said and gave her a high five.

She high-fived me back and said, "Now, let's hope we get on."

They started clearing standbys, and numbers one through three got on. Then they finally called our names: "Alejandra Sanchez, C. J. Nicholas?"

"Right here," we said.

We got the last two tickets, and the gate agent checked our IDs, handed us the tickets, and spotted our luggage. "You guys need to check your bags, and then leave them at the bottom of the jetway."

"No problem," we said, taking the tickets and running down the jetway to the plane. We dropped our luggage at the jetway door opposite the plane entrance and headed onto the plane. I was in 38B, and Alejandra was in 35B. We were away from each other, but, hey, we were on our way to Albuquerque. I wondered if I should call Bugs Bunny and tell him we'd be in town?

It was a five-hour flight to Albuquerque, and we slept. It was an uneventful flight, and we finally landed in New Mexico. After leaving the aircraft, we headed to baggage claim and waited for our luggage. And waited, and waited. Alejandra's black suitcase finally arrived with its pretty pink bow on it; then we were just waiting for mine.

"I'm going to the car rental desk. Meet me there once you get your luggage," Alejandra said.

"Okay, I'll see you soon," I replied and kissed her.

After fifteen minutes, I realized that my luggage didn't make the trip to Albuquerque, and I was mad—fuming. How hard is it to put a piece of luggage on a fucking plane?

Alejandra texted me, "What's taking so long?"

I replied, "I think Global lost my fucking luggage. Those fucking assholes."

She ran back over to the baggage rail and saw that my luggage was not there. Albuquerque Airport is not that big; in fact, it's pretty small. She saw my anger and said, "Look, I know that you're angry, but you can't be. They just took you to Albuquerque, New Mexico, for free. You have to be calm; otherwise, I can get in trouble since you're on my passes."

"Are you fucking kidding me?! I did nothing wrong! They lost my luggage, and now you're telling me I can't vent my frustration at the Global Airlines baggage claim?"

Alejandra got in my face and said sternly, "Yes, that's exactly what I am saying. Because if you go over there and rant and rave and carry on, the chances of you ever getting your luggage will be slim to none. And unless you want to buy a return ticket to Newark, then you need to stop!"

I was so pissed at Alejandra and the situation that I had to walk away from her.

"Where are you going?" she asked.

"I need to walk away right now. I'm fucking pissed off and need to get this off my chest or I'm going to hurt someone!"

"Fine, just meet me at the Hertz Car Rental when you're done with your tantrum," she said matter-of-factly.

I was going to rip someone's head off. I didn't care who the fuck it was. I was so pissed at her, Global Airlines, and the situation because I had only the clothes on my back for the week. I headed over to the Hertz Car Rental still angry as hell.

"Are we better?" she asked.

"No, I'm fucking not, Alejandra, and I'm not going to fucking calm down anytime soon," I replied. (I'm an English teacher; I swear with the best of them.)

"Well, you better because we need to go over to baggage claim to find out where your bags are. And we are not going over there with you like this," she said.

"Are you purposely trying to piss me off, or do you have this fantastic, innate ability to push my buttons today?" I said.

"Your call. We can wait here 'til you calm down, or we can go over there and then be on our way to El Paso. Our car is waiting. Don't be angry."

"Fine," I said through gritted teeth.

Alejandra gave me a kiss and took my hand. "Let's go. I'll do all the talking."

I should say that when I get mad, it takes me a while to calm down if I don't get it off my chest. When I don't get it off my chest, I get very short and curt with people. When I am extremely pissed off and haven't calmed down and can't let my frustration out, I internalize it, I get quiet, and I don't want to talk to you.

We headed over to the Global Airlines baggage claim, and Alejandra did all the talking, handed my baggage claim ticket to the baggage claim attendant, and learned that my bag was still in Newark in the jetway.

"When can we get it?" Alejandra asked the attendant.

"Is this your final destination?" she asked.

"No, El Paso," Alejandra said.

"Let me make a phone call. I'll ask," she said.

A couple of minutes later, the baggage claim attendant said, "Monday, the earliest."

"Okay, thank you. That will be fine," Alejandra replied.

"Just continue to call the baggage tracker number, and they'll give you updates," she said.

"Okay, thank you," we said and headed to the Hertz parking lot.

Alejandra rented a yellow 2005 Chevy Aveo. We put her luggage and my red backpack carry-on into the limited trunk space and got in. We left the parking lot and made a left out of the parking lot to head on I-10 east for a three-and-a-half hour car ride. But before we hit the road, we pulled into a Whataburger to get lunch.

Alejandra was talking a mile a minute and was so excited about heading home. I, on the other hand, had not said two words to her since we were with the baggage claim attendant.

"What's wrong?" she asked.

"Nothing," I replied tersely, which signals to anyone on the planet that something is wrong.

"Is it the lost luggage?" Alejandra asked.

"This isn't the place to hash this out," I said curtly.

"You're blaming me?" she asked.

"Again, I'm not doing this here," I said shortly.

"Fine," Alejandra said abruptly.

We finished our lunch in silence and headed to the Wha-taburger parking lot to get into our rental car. I pulled out of the parking lot and headed onto I-10. I-10 is the hypnosis highway; it's just straight for three and a half hours going right through the desert. There were hardly any cars on the road. It was 12 p.m. mountain time. Since I'm from New Jersey and traffic and toll booths are a way of life, this was a breeze. Except I was pissed off at Alejandra for not letting me vent my frustration at the airport.

"I'm not sitting in silence for three and a half hours, C. J., so you'd better tell me what's going on," she said angrily.

"Okay, I'm pissed off at your company for losing my luggage; I'm pissed off at you because you wouldn't let me vent my frus-tration at baggage claim and for telling me to stifle my emotions because you can get into trouble if I get angry. When can I get mad? Never. Just take it. Well, I'm not built that way, and if the shoe was on the other foot, you would have given the baggage claim attendant a piece of your mind!"

Alejandra said, "Look, I'm sorry if you wanted to vent, but I'm not losing my job for anyone. I understand that you are angry that they lost your luggage, but Global Airlines took you here for free."

"I'm sorry, but when I'm mad, I need an outlet to vent, and you would not give me one, and that was making me angrier by the second. I apologize."

"I'm sorry too, babe," and she leaned over and gave me a quick kiss on the cheek since we were traveling at seventy miles per hour

Like any fight, it's not over until the make-up sex happens, and considering we were driving on I-10, I was thinking *tonight*.

"I can give you an outlet right now, if you want?" she said, seductively leaning into my ear.

"There is no place to pull over," I said.

She then proceeded to unzip the fly of my pants, and I quickly understood what she meant. "Don't get into an accident," she said.

"I won't," I said and then received one of the best blow jobs I have ever had while driving seventy-five miles per hour on I-10.

Alejandra was sucking my dick so well I could hardly concentrate on the road. I increased my speed to eighty miles per hour while she was blowing me.

Once we were done, everything went back to normal, and we were talking and singing to the radio. Tension released. Who knew?

I-10 has now become my all-time favorite highway in America, and to this day, anytime I drive on it—which is quite often considering my in-laws live in El Paso and this is the main road through that city—I think about this spectacular event.

Three-and-a-half hours later, we arrived in El Paso at her sister's house. We got out of the car, stretched our legs, and entered the modest, white ranch home. Suzanne was more than welcoming to this stranger who was dating her sister, and she was quite cute too. She was short, 125 pounds, had long brown hair, brown eyes, and a nice little figure (not that I'm noticing, Alejandra; just describing her to the readers). We put Alejandra's luggage and my backpack into the guest room and proceeded to go directly to Target because I obviously needed clothes. Suzanne came with us to catch up with her sister and maybe to feel out what type of guy I was.

We parked in the Target parking lot and headed in so I could shop. I should explain that if I had gone into the store by myself, I would have been out in ten minutes. But anytime I go shopping with Alejandra, it's going to be an hour, because she is going to dress me and make me try out any and every outfit that she thinks will look good on me. So we bought two sets of jeans, a couple of shirts, and a twelve-pack of colored boxer briefs.

We headed back to Suzanne's place and showered—individually, of course—and I changed into my new clothes. We had dinner and drinks and a good time.

The next day, I called for my luggage and found out it was in Denver on its way to El Paso. I thought, great, I should have it by this afternoon. Yeah, that's a nice assumption, C. J., but this is Global Airlines, and in reality, that doesn't happen. I called in the afternoon: still in Denver. I called in the evening and asked to speak with a customer service person and not a machine. The conversation went something like this:

"Customer Service, how can I help you?"

"Yes, my name is C. J. Nicholas, and my baggage claim number is 345972."

"Hi, Mr. Nicholas. I have located your luggage. It's currently at Denver International Airport ready for pickup."

"That's great, cause I'm in El Paso," I said sarcastically. "It was supposed to be sent to El Paso, Texas."

"Mr. Nicholas, we do not have that on our direction screen. It says Denver."

"Let me get this straight: I travelled to Albuquerque Airport, and you guys sent my luggage to Denver, expecting me to pick it up there, when I specifically told you that my final destination is El Paso, Texas, when I landed in Albuquerque," I exclaimed.

"I guess we made a mistake, Mr. Nicholas," said the customer service agent.

"You guess? You do know Denver is in Colorado, Albuquerque is in New Mexico, and El Paso is in Texas? I don't need to send you a map of the continental United States, but I will if you need me to. What are the chances I get my luggage before the end of the week?" I asked again sarcastically.

"The earliest I can get it to El Paso is if I put a rush on it, Wednesday."

"Put the rush on it, please," I said.

"Your confirmation number is AZ543."

"Thanks," I said, and hung up.

Alejandra asked me, "What happened?"

"I'm convinced your company has a team of monkeys running it. My luggage is in Denver, and long story short, the earliest it's going to be here is Wednesday."

"Wednesday? Why is it in Denver?" she asked.

"These are great questions. Apparently, they never put my final destination as El Paso when we left the baggage claim in Albuquerque. That's why it's in Denver." I was frustrated.

"Well, you have clothes. We can just wash them every other day so you got something to wear until Wednesday," Alejandra said.

Wednesday finally arrived, and I got a text alerting me that my luggage was in El Paso, Texas.

Alejandra and I took the rental car to El Paso Airport, found their baggage claim, and finally picked up my blue roller board with the football luggage tag. I turned to Alejandra and said, "Finally. Next time, I'm yelling at the baggage claim attendant."

6

Tucson, Arizona

I MENTIONED TO ALEJANDRA ONE day that we could make some easy money off her being a flight attendant.

"How?" she asked.

"With a simple bet," I said.

"Bet?"

"Yes. You are a very attractive woman, and men look at you in my presence. If I see this on a plane, I'll bet the guy a hundred bucks that I can get your number before he can. You give me your number and blow him off. When I flick the side of my nose with my index finger, you know the bet is on. Easy money." The flick of the index finger is from the movie *The Sting*. I demonstrated so that she'd recognize the signal and give it back. We are really clandestine.

She laughed and said, "Okay, when we're on a flight, correct?"

"Correct," I said.

Flashforward to 2008: I had proposed to Alejandra in June of 2007, and we were getting married two months from then in

El Paso. It was the beginning of February and fucking cold in the New York/New Jersey area, where snow piles on every street corner around three feet high from the previous snowstorm. Looking to get out of the area and visit a warmer climate, I was looking on Alejandra's company website for flights that she could work and I could get on as a passenger. I came across a two-day Tucson trip that left Newark on Friday, February 8, at 9 p.m. and left Tucson at 9 p.m. on Saturday. We'd have all day Sunday to sleep and relax in Jersey City.

"Alejandra, I think I found a trip for us!" I said proudly.

"Where?"

"Tucson, Arizona," I said.

"What the hell is in Tucson?"

"Eighty-degree weather in February, a pool, and a reprieve from the igloo that we're currently stuck in."

"Give me the computer," she said.

She looked and found a position available in first-class, then looked at the flight. It was wide open both coming and going, and so was first class. If she took the position, she would be my personal flight attendant (porn fantasy fulfilled).

"Okay, I'll do it." Alejandra clicked on the position and then listed me for first class on that same flight.

I was first on the list of standbys with no problem getting there or getting back. And for the first time in our relationship, Alejandra was going to be my personal flight attendant. Two words: *giggity giggity*.

Friday came and went at school, and we headed to the airport, no rush. The flight was at 9 p.m., and we arrived at the airport with plenty of time. We had dinner at the food court and then walked to our gate. Alejandra got on with the crew, gave me a kiss, winked, and said, "See you inside, Mr. Papagiorgio."

I smiled and waited for them to call my name for First Class. Since the flight was wide open, I headed over to the gate agent and told her, "I'm standby passenger C. J. Nicholas."

"Yes, Mr. Nicholas, here's your ticket. Enjoy your flight."

"I will, thank you," I replied.

While waiting to board the plane, I noticed four gentlemen with Colorado Rockies carry-on bags. They looked athletic, like baseball players. I put one and one together and realized they were headed to spring training in Tucson, Arizona.

They called first-class passengers, military personnel, and families with children under the age of two to board the plane first. Since I knew I was getting first class, I was dressed in khaki pants, black leather loafers, and a light blue button down. I walked onto the plane and was greeted by the most beautiful flight attendant in the fleet. "Good evening, sir, may I see your ticket?" Alejandra asked.

Once again, we were playing the "I'm a perfect stranger" game. I handed her my ticket.

"1A, right here, sir. Would you like something to drink?"

"Yes, vodka and Sprite, please," I said.

"Right away, sir," she said.

I wondered if I could get this service at home: "Alejandra, I'd like a blow job."

"Right away, sir."

I'd try it on Sunday.

The seat next to me was empty as people boarded the flight. I was thinking, not only am I getting first class, but no one is sitting next to me. Extra room to spread out. Bonus! The most beautiful flight attendant in the fleet brought over my vodka and Sprite, and I was feeling pretty good about myself.

The gate agent walked onto the plane, went through first

class, and came back with a rather large gentleman. She parked him in seat 1B, right next to me. He was six-and-a-half feet tall, 240 pounds, athletic, and wearing a red flannel shirt, blue jeans, and cowboy boots. "Thank God. My legs were up against the seat in front of me in coach," he said in his Texas drawl. "Josh Johnson." He extended his paw of a hand.

I shook it and said, "C. J. Nicholas."

"Nice meeting you. Why you headed to Tucson?" he asked.

"A little R and R," I said. "You?"

"Work. I'm a pitcher for the Rockies headed to Spring Training," Josh stated proudly.

"Nice. Good luck. I'll look for you in the sports pages this season," I said, secretly jealous because he was living out a boyhood dream of mine. Hell, if I was playing baseball for a Major League team, I would have put it on a T-shirt.

"Excuse me, gentlemen, but would you like something to drink?" Alejandra said to Josh.

"A beer," he replied.

"What kind?" she asked politely.

"Budweiser."

"Right away." She turned around and headed back to the galley. As she turned, Josh checked out her ass.

Immediately, I thought, "Okay, asshole, you asked for this. The bet is on. I hope Alejandra remembers."

"She's beautiful," I said.

"Yeah, she's cute," Josh said.

"I got an idea, since we both think she's good looking. I bet a hundred bucks that I can get her number before you."

He looked at me, laughed, and said, "Sure. But let me see the cash first."

I pulled out my wallet and revealed five twenty-dollar bills.

"And you?"

He opened his wallet and pulled out a hundred-dollar bill.

"Okay, so when she comes back, it starts," I declared.

"Sure. The easiest hundred bucks I ever made," Josh proclaimed.

Alejandra came back with the beer, and I flicked the side of my nose with my index finger, giving her the signal that the bet was now on.

She saw the signal and smiled at us both. Josh went into some spiel about how he was a big-league baseball player, and how long she was in town in Tucson.

"Just for the weekend. Why?" Alejandra asked.

"I was wondering if you'd like to come by the ballpark and watch me pitch. Then we can get dinner afterward," Josh said confidently.

"I'm sorry, sir, but I'm not allowed to fraternize with the passengers socially. Company policy," she stated politely.

"You can't break company policy?" he asked.

"Sorry, sir," Alejandra said.

During this whole conversation, I was looking at my TV screen, trying not to laugh and feigning interest.

"Excuse me, sir, would you like another drink?" Alejandra asked me.

"Yes, ma'am, please," I said.

She turned and walked away to get my drink, and Josh said, "Good luck, buddy. You're gonna need it."

Alejandra came back with my drink and said, "Would you like anything else?"

"Not right now, thank you, though," I said.

She left, and Josh turned to me and said, "Candy ass."

"Just biding my time," I said.

An hour into the flight, I saw Alejandra and said, "May I ask you something?"

She said, "It depends."

"Well, I know it's against company policy to go out to dinner with a customer, but you have the most beautiful elbows I have ever seen on a woman, and I can't take my eyes off them. Can I ask you for a drink after the flight? I'm staying at the Tucson Hilton."

Alejandra cracked up. "How can I turn down that offer? And what a coincidence. I'm staying there too."

"Give me your number, and I'll meet you at the hotel bar," I said to her. She wrote her name and number on a napkin.

"Give me an hour after we land, then you can call me."

"Sure," I said.

Josh's jaw dropped. In disbelief, he asked her, "Him, really? Him?"

Alejandra said, "I'll give you three reasons why: one, he's good looking; two, he's funny; and three and most importantly, he's nice."

Check and mate. She left, and I turned to Josh. "I believe you owe me some money."

He took out his wallet and handed me the hundred-dollar bill. "I can't believe I lost to you."

"Hey, you're lucky we didn't compare dick sizes. Otherwise, you might have to retreat back to economy class," I said.

He laughed and said, "She's right—you are funny."

To sum up, the bet worked, and we were a hundred dollars richer. Sorry, Josh, but I'm from Jersey, and I have never been a fan of arrogant assholes.

We landed in Tucson, and Josh left first. I waited at the top of the jetway for my fiancée. I met the crew, and Alejandra introduced me, this time for real, as her fiancé. Then we headed to the white crew van outside the airport. The van driver (let's call him Robert) carried a white sign with the flight number written on it: *Flight 834 Crew*.

We headed to the back of the van, handed the van driver our luggage, and he put it in the back of the van. The ride from Tucson Airport to the Hilton was thirty minutes, and the crew made small talk. I kept my mouth shut. We reached the hotel and headed to the back of the van to retrieve our luggage. Robert got out and started taking out everyone's luggage, everyone's except Alejandra's.

"Where's my black roller board?" she asked Robert.

"What black roller board?" Robert replied.

"The black roller board I handed you back at the airport," Alejandra said, getting her Latina up. "You left it there? I can't believe you left it there!" She started to yell. Immediately, the lead flight attendant, Erin, came over and asked Alejandra what was going on.

"He lost my roller board," she said to Erin, pointing to Robert.

"Okay, let's get our hotel keys. Then we'll go back to the airport, and hopefully we can find it," Erin said.

"Stay with him," Alejandra yelled at me. "Make sure he doesn't go anywhere. He's taking us back to the airport!"

I looked at that poor bastard Robert, and I knew exactly what was about to happen to him on this thirty-minute trip back to the airport. Alejandra was about to go full Latina Ricky-Ricardo-machine-gun Spanish on his ass, and there was nothing anyone could do to stop it.

Alejandra and Erin got the hotel keys and came back to the white van. Erin was a nice lady about fifty, reddish brown hair, blue eyes, nice figure, average height, 130 pounds, and Irish. She insisted on coming with us. The more the merrier.

Robert was in his early twenties, Hispanic, black hair, brown eyes, just taller than Erin, 150 pounds, and very slim build. We got in the van, and we weren't even out of the hotel driveway before Alejandra started in on Robert. "How can you lose a bag

I handed you? Do you know what happens to an unaccompanied bag at the airport? They blow it up! Do you know what happens to me? I can be fined $10,000 and be fired!" She was yelling at Robert, browbeating him like no tomorrow.

While Alejandra went on, an idea popped into my head: she didn't let me vent when my luggage got lost in Albuquerque. What is it that she said? Don't be angry.

Immediately, I got a Grinch-like smile on my face and said to Alejandra, "Honey, don't be angry."

She looked at me and yelled, "Shut the fuck up, C. J.!"

"What did I do? I'm just telling you not to be angry." I feigned disgust.

"I know exactly what you're doing, Mister." Then she went full Latina and Ricky Ricardo on me, spewing a slew of Spanish curse words and ending in *pinche guero*.

"You are so fucking hot right now. I swear if we were in the hotel room, I would be all over you like a cheap suit," I said.

Steam was now escaping from her ears. More Spanish at me.

We arrived at the airport, and Erin and Alejandra went back into the Tucson Airport Security Desk to explain how Robert left her roller board at the curb. TSA took Erin and Alejandra in the back because they had airport credentials and showed Alejandra her bag. "We x-rayed your bag," said the TSA agent. "We found nothing that was contraband, so we figured you would come back for it."

"Thank God you didn't blow it up," Alejandra said, relieved.

They got the bag, and we headed back to the white van and Robert. Alejandra brought the bag into the van with her rather than trusting Robert. Once bitten, twice shy. She proceeded to go through it and double check that everything was in it, which it was.

I said, "It feels good to vent, right?"

She looked at me angrily and said, "Yes."

"Remember in Albuquerque when you wouldn't let me do this? That's all I wanted to do," I said.

Lesson learned.

We finally arrived back at the hotel. It was now 2 a.m. mountain time, and we'd spent two hours traveling back and forth to the airport. We exited the white van and didn't tip Robert. We thanked Erin for coming with us and headed to our rooms. I swept the room and nodded for Alejandra to come in. Then we jumped into the shower to get the airplane gunk off and headed to bed.

We woke at noon the next day and had brunch at the hotel restaurant. After all, it was on Josh. After brunch, we headed back to the room to get into our bathing suits to spend a couple of hours at the pool, work on our tans, and enjoy the eighty-degree weather in February. Alejandra had this blue bikini on, and I had blue swim trunks and a white T-shirt. She brought her straw sunhat and sunglasses, and I had my sunglasses and white Nike visor.

We waited for the elevator because we were on the ninth floor, then got on it when it finally arrived at our floor. Alejandra hit the "G" button for the ground floor. The elevator doors closed, and we started to descend. It stopped at the fifth floor and opened. Standing in front of us was Robert the van driver. He saw us and said, "I'll take the next one," and waited for the doors to shut again.

Alejandra looked at me and said, "I can't believe he would not ride the elevator with us."

"You did verbally ride him like Seabiscuit last night," I said.

"I should apologize to him," she said.

"Good luck with that," I said. "Let it be." And we headed to the pool.

7

Lisbon, Portugal

ALEJANDRA AND I GOT MARRIED in April of 2008, and it was a beautiful wedding. Normally, couples go on their honeymoon right after their wedding. Unfortunately, we were both teachers and could not do so until the end of the school year in June. So we decided to buy full-fare tickets (so we wouldn't get bumped) to Lisbon, Portugal, for ten days the following August.

The day before our honeymoon, we went to a carnival in Oakland, New Jersey, to visit my sister and her kids, who were three and one years old at the time. We had an enjoyable time watching our niece and nephew ride all the kiddie rides. We also had dinner there. The carnival was like any other carnival that came to town; it took over a ballfield, or a series of ballfields, for the week. The food was made by volunteers at little outdoor booths. They had the usual items: burgers, hot dogs, chicken. I had two cheeseburgers at the carnival and thought nothing of it . . .

... until ten o'clock that night. This was when I was projectile-vomiting and having diarrhea at the same time. I couldn't keep anything in me. I was literally sitting on a toilet and throwing up in a bag at the same time all night. I got no sleep whatsoever. At six the next morning, I was so exhausted from throwing up and pooping my brains out that I finally crawled into bed. Alejandra felt my head and said I had also developed a fever. I was shaking. I woke up at 11 a.m. to throw up one more time, brush my teeth, then go back to bed. Alejandra called her sister, Suzanne.

"He is really sick, Suzanne."

"Take him to the hospital," Suzanne said. "It sounds like he has food poisoning."

"We are leaving for our honeymoon tonight, Sue!" Alejandra said.

"See if the airline will exchange your tickets for tomorrow. He needs to rest," Sue said.

"Good idea. I'm calling them now. Bye, Suzie," Alejandra answered.

She immediately called Global Airlines and spoke to someone in Customer Service after going through the mandatory screening of robot voices and ten minutes of waiting. "Yes, hi, my name is Alejandra Nicholas, and I am a flight attendant for our airline. My husband and I are going on our honeymoon to Lisbon, and we bought full-fare tickets. He has food poisoning, and we were wondering if we could switch our tickets to tomorrow?"

After five minutes, the customer service representative got back on the line and said, "Ma'am, I can switch your ticket to tomorrow for $2,000."

Alejandra replied, "Really? Okay, we'll stick with the original flight."

She turned to me, still shivering in bed. "We're going. It's

$2,000 to change the flight to tomorrow, and we don't have that money. Sleep till 4 p.m., and we'll leave at 5 p.m. for our 9 p.m. flight."

I just nodded my head and passed out in bed.

She woke me up at four to shower. I was still shivering and feeling as if someone had run over me with an 18-wheeler, backed up, and run over me again. At 4 p.m., Alejandra drove us to the airport. We hit the usual rush hour traffic, but our flight wasn't until 9 p.m., so we were not worried about it. Of course, I slept the entire ride to Newark Airport. We parked in the employee lot and waited for the bus to come. The bus came and again we waited for the people to get off first because they had the right of way. We got on the bus, and the other employees were looking at me as if I were one of the living dead. I was pale, feverish, and just miserable, while Alejandra was playing Nurse Ratchett and driving me like a husky sled dog. We got through security and waited outside the gate. I was sitting in a chair, huddled in a ball shivering. Alejandra saw me and said, "I'll go get you some Tylenol."

"Okay," I said weakly.

I looked across from me, and there was some teenager taking a photo of me because of how miserable I looked. I proceeded to give him the finger and told him, "Come closer. I'm highly contagious."

He left. Fucking millennials.

Alejandra came back with some Tylenol and water. I popped two of them in my mouth. She saw me shivering and asked, "Do you want me to get you a sweatshirt?"

"I'll go and get it," I said.

I walked gingerly to an airport souvenir stand and purchased a dark-blue Yankee Stadium crewneck sweatshirt. (This was the last season in the Old Yankee Stadium. In 2009, the Yankees built a new one.) I immediately put the sweatshirt on and walked back to Alejandra. I sat next to her and closed my eyes. It was a weird feeling paying for tickets and knowing we were going to make the flight. There was no mystery, nervousness, excitement, relief—how boring.

We were in Group 3 of the boarding process and waited in line. They scanned our tickets, and we boarded the plane. Alejandra gave me the aisle seat, 22A, just in case I had to run to the bathroom and vomit. She sat in 22B. I slept with Alejandra next to me, her head on my shoulder to join me, and the flight took off for Portugal.

Around 1 a.m., I felt a constant nudging on my left shoulder that woke me out of a deep slumber. It was Alejandra, and she looked distressed. "What's up?" I asked groggily.

"Someone took my glasses," she said frantically.

"And that's all they touched?" I said sarcastically.

"I mean it. Someone took my eyeglasses."

"Where were they?" I asked

"Hooked on my shirt," she said. "Look under your seat."

I should preface that Alejandra is as blind as a bat without her glasses or contacts. I carefully checked by my feet and under my seat. They weren't there. Alejandra asked me to get up, because I apparently didn't do a good enough job to her high standards of searching.

She was now on the ground looking for her glasses like Velma from Scooby-Doo. She woke up the poor gentlemen sitting on her left and asked him if he could check by his area. I was now standing in the aisle. Two flight attendants came over to us and asked, "What's going on?"

Alejandra said, "I lost my glasses. I can't find them anywhere. They were hooked on my shirt, but now they're gone."

Both flight attendants got their pocket flashlights, and Alejandra and the two of them proceed to wake up everyone in a three-row radius. Mindy, one of the flight attendants, found them three rows behind us near 25B.

Alejandra was excited and took them from Mindy. "Thank you."

She then put her glasses away in their case. She sat back in her seat, gave me a kiss on the cheek, put her eye shades over her eyes, and went back to sleep.

Meanwhile, all three rows in our radius were looking at me with hatred for waking them up. My wife, Alejandra, contently passed out on my shoulder.

After an hour, I went back to sleep, and was awakened later by Alejandra saying, "We're descending; we're almost there. How do you feel?"

"Better, but I think I should stick to water, and not eat anything," I said.

The flight attendants come around with orange juice and croissants, and immediately my stomach craved them because I hadn't eaten anything for close to twenty-four hours.

Alejandra said, "Try to have a croissant. You need to eat something, and it's not heavy."

"Okay, I'll try." I literally devoured the croissant in two bites.

"Hungry?" she asked sarcastically.

"I would eat yours, but I don't want to have another stomach episode," I said.

We landed and headed to baggage claim in Lisbon Portela Airport. The baggage-claim area is a huge room with white linoleum floor. We collected our luggage and got in line for a cab to take us to our hotel. Unlike "Hotel Sticky Door" in Paris, we were staying at a three-star hotel in the center of Lisbon. The concierge was a man in his late thirties, balding, with glasses and a little heavyset build. His name was Joao. Joao gave us the keys to our hotel room, and the bellhop brought our luggage to our room. We crossed the black marble floor to the elevators and arrived on the fourth floor. The bellhop opened our door without having to dislocate his shoulder. He brought our luggage in, I tipped him, and Alejandra and I showered in a shower which had a curtain to contain the water. We then went to bed and slept to adjust to the time change.

We woke up and got dressed. I wore a short-sleeved blue T-shirt and green shorts and flip flops; Alejandra wore a white blouse, red and black striped skirt, and flip flops. We headed downstairs and asked Joao where we should eat, since Alejandra liked to eat where the locals eat.

Joao said, "Well, it's a little bit away. You would have to take the metro for a couple of stops, but it's a very good restaurant, and it's by the Santa Justa Elevator."

"Okay, sounds great," Alejandra said excitedly.

Joao gave us directions, and we walked about three blocks to the metro. The metro station was filled with shops, restaurants, and tons of people. We bought our tickets and read the board to find out which train to take. We rode the metro for three stops and got off. We walked up the steps and now had to figure out in which direction the restaurant was. We made a right and headed towards the sea, apparently in the wrong direction, as we soon found out. After being lost for fifteen minutes, Alejandra asked one of the locals, in Spanish, since neither of us can speak Portuguese, "Where is this restaurant?" She pointed to a piece of paper Joao had given us with the name and address on it.

The local, an older gentleman in his sixties, answered in Spanish, "About two blocks from the Santa Justa Elevator." He pointed in the direction we'd just come from.

Alejandra said, "*Gracias.*"

We went back the way we came and passed the 150-foot Santa Justa Elevator, which is very tall and skinny and looks a lot like a miniature Eiffel Tower. As it turned out, the man who created it was a student of Gustave Eiffel. The line was very short since it was seven at night, and Alejandra and I decided to pay the €1.50 each to go to the top. We rode the narrow elevator to the observation deck and saw a beautiful view of Portugal. As the great Daniel Craig says in *Skyfall*, "Never waste a view."

After ten minutes of breathtaking views of Lisbon, we traveled back down the elevator, made a left, and finally headed to the restaurant. We found the street it was on and walked in. It was empty. Great call, Joao. We saw the proprietor, and Alejandra asked him in Spanish, "Are you open?"

"*Sí, sí,*" the owner said enthusiastically.

"Joao recommended us to you, from our hotel, Hotel Tejo," Alejandra said in Spanish.

"Ah, tell Joao I said hello and thank you," said the owner.

He sat us by the window, obviously to show other customers that he was open. He handed us our menus which had an English translation. I ordered fish, and Alejandra did the same.

We made some small talk while we waited for our food to arrive.

"How's your stomach?" Alejandra asked.

"Much better," I replied.

Our food arrived, and it was delicious. Again, I devoured mine because I hadn't eaten since the plane. Alejandra daintily ate hers. I paid for the meal, and we started to walk slowly back to the metro to enjoy the shops and the scenery. We got back on the metro and went to our hotel. Joao was not there when we walked in, so we went to the hotel bar for a drink and to come up with a plan for the following day.

I ordered a vodka and sprite, and Alejandra ordered a glass of wine. Our plan was to spend two days at the beach in Cascais and Costa de Caparica, one day in Sintra, one day in Fatima, one day in Barrio Alto, one day at Rossio Square, and three days in Lisbon visiting all the sights.

"So where to tomorrow?" I asked.

"How about the beach? Cascais?" Alejandra said.

"Sure," I said.

We asked the bartender how to get to Cascais.

The bartender, a slender man in his fifties, said, "You need to take a train to get there. It's about an hour and a half away. So get there early."

"Okay," Alejandra said.

We headed back to the room, and Alejandra set the alarm for 7:30 a.m. so we could get ready and catch the metro to the 8:20 a.m. train for Cascais.

We woke up, dressed in our bathing suits, and headed downstairs to catch the metro to the train to Cascais. Alejandra was wearing a white bikini, blue cover up, straw sunhat, and sunglasses and carrying a straw beach bag with our towels and suntan lotion. I was wearing blue swim trunks, a white T-shirt, white Nike visor, and flip flops.

As we headed out, we saw Joao and told him we had a great time at the restaurant and that we were headed to Cascais for the day.

We took the metro and then the train for the hour-and-a-half ride to Cascais. The ride was easy and relaxing. We arrived in Cascais along with the other beachgoers. We literally stepped off the train, and there it was: the beach. The train pulled out, and we walked about three hundred feet to the beach. The Cascais beaches weren't like the Jersey Shore beaches, which are flat. There were small hills that required stairs to get to the beach. We walked to the steps and descended to the beach. On my right were four young women about the age of twenty-five, completely topless, and lying on their towels. They could have been models. God, I love Europe.

As we searched for a spot to put down our beach blanket, I noticed there were many topless women. God bless the European culture. Unfortunately, Alejandra noticed me noticing the topless women. "Oh, you like her? Do you want to sit next to her and stare at her tits while you get a suntan?" she said angrily.

Alejandra is self-conscious about her breasts. I don't understand why. I think they're perfect. But ever since I have dated her, she has been this way. I said, "Sure, why not." I shrugged and set the beach bag on the sand.

"Is this what you want, you want to look at tits?" She angrily took off her top for all the world to see.

True genius has never been appreciated during its time, and apparently my excellent plan worked. How do you get your new wife out of her bathing suit top? Just stare at someone else's breasts and she'll get so mad that she'll take off her top. Pure genius, guys. You may want to try this when you're in Europe.

I smiled and told her, "I love your tits, and I'll show you later." I kissed her hard on the mouth.

"You better," she said.

We put suntan lotion on each other and sat and relaxed on the beach. After a while, I started getting hot and decided to go in the water. It was low tide, so we had to walk out about 150 yards to get into hip-deep water. I said, "I'm going in the water. I'm hot, and since I have been on the other side of the Atlantic,

I might as well try this side."

"Okay, love," Alejandra said.

Alejandra doesn't like the water; in fact, I have never seen her swim. I did the five-toe test, and the water was cold, probably around sixty-five degrees to my guesstimation. I reached the bippy point on my swim trunks and let out a yell of, "Cold!" I decided on five minutes in, tops. I dove into a wave, popped up, and turned toward the shore. I got the ocean water out of my eyes and whom did I see but one of the twenty-five-year-old models diving through the same wave as I just had. She popped up from the water, and it was Tits A'hoy! A 36-D easy (not that I was measuring them, Alejandra, just admiring them). This woman (let's call her Ines) was tall, thin, tan, brown-eyed and brown-haired, and wearing a red bikini.

When I saw her, I smiled and said to myself, *I think I'm in here a little bit longer.* Ines was now trying to ride the waves and doing a terrible job at it, but who was I to tell her she was doing it wrong? I mean, I could bodysurf with anyone and get beached almost every time. But I was just going to let her get up and watch her tits bounce up and down like any good man would.

I'd been in the water for over a half an hour. My lips were probably blue, and my body felt and looked like Jack's at the end of the movie *Titanic*. I finally listened to my body and got out of the water and went back to Alejandra and our blanket.

"Where have you been? Your lips are blue, and you're shivering," Alejandra asked.

"The water is invigorating," I stated, shivering with a towel over my shoulders. "I was bodysurfing."

"Right," Alejandra said skeptically.

I started to warm up, put my sunglasses on, and watched Ines get out of the water and walk over to her hot model friends about a hundred yards away from our blanket.

It was about noon when Alejandra said, "Do you want to get lunch? I'm hungry, and I saw a restaurant overlooking the beach when we walked in."

"Sure," I said.

Alejandra put her top back on and her blue cover up. We left our blankets and towels and took our beach bag. On the way up the stairs, I noticed Ines and her friends, still topless, playing paddle ball. Was this heaven? Was I dead? Was someone doing compressions on my chest? This couldn't be real, could it?

Alejandra saw what, or rather, whom I was looking at and said, "Come on. Let's go. Nothing to see here."

Now I was pulling an "Alejandra," turning around every twenty feet and admiring the view of two beautiful women playing topless paddle ball and going, "Wow!"

Alejandra literally grabbed me by the hand and dragged me to the restaurant. We sat outside, and Alejandra strategically positioned me with my back to Ines and her friend. Just kill my view, why don't you.

We ordered lunch and some drinks. Alejandra said, "So when did you spot them?" She pointed to Ines and her friend.

"The moment we got on the beach," I said.

"Uh-huh," she said. "And let me guess—that's why you were in the ocean so long."

I knew I was in trouble here; no use lying to a Latina about it. Lying will always make it worse. Just admit it and take the machine-gun Spanish that's heading your way. "Well, as you saw from my body, the water was cold, and when I jumped into a wave and came up, the one in the red bikini bottom was three feet away from me. I decided then and there to stay in the ocean, as a former lifeguard, to make sure she was okay."

Alejandra burst out laughing. "Really, just her."

"Yes, as I said before, I'm a former lifeguard [I really am], and I'm not on duty, but I watched her, and she didn't look like such a strong swimmer. So I decided to stay and make sure in case I had to pull her up from under the water," I said matter-of-factly.

"By her breasts, I'm sure," Alejandra said.

"By whatever means necessary. But you're right, most likely by her breasts," I said.

"You know we are on our honeymoon?"

"I know, and there is no one else but you, but if you let me, I'll go down there and invite them all back to our place for a drink, and we'll see what happens from there," I replied.

"You do that, and I'm going to take my steak knife here and cut it off," she said, smiling.

Sleep with one eye open tonight, C. J. I laughed nervously; I knew that she would do it. She's hotblooded and passionate. That's why I love her so much.

"I'm sorry, love, for admiring the view. I apologize."

"You better be," she said seriously.

"I will tonight," I said seductively, hoping to turn the tables and parlay this into some sex later tonight.

We finished our lunch and spent a couple more hours on the beach, then hit the shops of Cascais. Alejandra knows I hate to shop, so she parked me at an Irish bar, of all places in Portugal. She's a smart woman. I had a beer while she shopped for an hour.

Alejandra came back after I had a couple of beers and felt pretty good. We held hands on our way back to the train and made small talk about the day at Cascais.

"Did you enjoy the beach?" Alejandra said.

"Immensely."

"I'm sure."

We got off the train and took the metro back to our stop, then took the three-block walk hand in hand. We crossed the marble floor of the hotel to the elevators, reached our floor and our room, and I attacked her.

"You better make this up to me," she said.

"Oh, don't you worry. I plan on apologizing to you all night." I unclasped her bikini top and started playing with her breasts and nipples.

She let out a small moan, grabbed my dick, and unbuttoned my bathing suit to stroke it quickly. We headed to the shower because we had all the beach gunk on us—seawater, suntan lotion, and sand. We entered the water and quickly went back at it. I washed all the important areas on Alejandra—tits, pussy, and ass. She continued to stroke my rock-hard cock. I bent her over, and we started to fuck in the shower doggie style. The water was hot and fantastic, and so was her body.

We got out of the shower, toweled off, and I continued apologizing for the rest of the night . . . and honeymoon.

By the way, it was a fantastic honeymoon.

8

Amsterdam, Netherlands

TWO WORDS ABOUT AMSTERDAM: *FUCKING BRRRR.* In January of 2009, Alejandra and I decided to go away for the Martin Luther King, Jr., three-day holiday. Of course, in my district, they gave the kids off, but the teachers had to go to work for in-service day. Six hours of wishing you were somewhere else. They do this because we get professional hours. In New Jersey, we need twenty professional hours for the academic year, so six hours is huge. But since I was going for my master's degree online at the time, I had sixty hours in January already, so I needed hours like I needed another hole in my head. Alejandra, whose attitude was "Fuck them; if you died tomorrow, they would replace you before your obituary was printed," suggested we go to Amsterdam for a long three-day weekend.

As always, I said, "Sure."

Two days before the trip, Alejandra bought me long underwear. I gave her a puzzled look.

She said, "It's incredibly cold over there—like ten below. You're going to thank me."

Alejandra knew I hate the cold.

I replied, "Why don't we go somewhere tropical?"

"This is culture. Plus, it's Europe and time to be with each other before the baby gets here," she said.

Alejandra was one month pregnant with our son, Jack, who would be born in August. "It was just a suggestion," I claimed.

As always, we would leave Friday night and land Saturday morning in Amsterdam, Netherlands. Alejandra booked a small hotel on the outskirts of the city called the Apple Inn.

We got on the flight and sat in coach. No chance for first class, but it was an uneventful flight. We landed, went through customs, got our passports stamped, and were about to take a taxi to our hotel when we stepped outside Amsterdam Airport Schipol. We were immediately greeted by the cold. It hit me like a ton of bricks. Eight below with a nice wind chill of negative fifteen. Balmy, if you're a polar bear or Mr. Freeze. Oh, and we had to wait for a cab in the elements, fan-fucking-tastic. After ten minutes and now entering my third stage of hypothermia, we got into a nice, warm taxi.

"Apple Inn, and take your time. We need to thaw out," I said.

The cabbie laughed and said, "Sure," in his Dutch accent. We arrived at the Apple Inn fifteen minutes later.

As we checked in, I asked the concierge if they had Wi-Fi.

"No, sir, I'm sorry, but there are plenty of internet cafes around the city," she stated.

"Okay," I said to the nice concierge, but I thought, "What hotel doesn't have Wi-Fi? Get into the now."

We entered our room on the second floor, and I completed the sweep of the room as Alejandra waited outside. I told her it was clear. We walked in, locked the door, and put our luggage in the quaint room. We undressed to get the airplane gunk off and slept to adjust to the time change.

We woke up at 4 p.m. Amsterdam time and quickly changed into our long johns and winter gear. We stepped outside the Apple Inn and were immediately met by the ferocious wind and negative temperatures. "Holy shit, it's fucking cold," I yelled to Alejandra through the wind.

"Aren't you glad I brought the long johns?" she said.

"Glad? I'm thrilled."

We walked towards the Amsterdam Tram stop and waited ten minutes. When the tram finally arrived, we'd enter our second stage of hypothermia. The blast of heat in the tram was incredible and such a welcomed relief from the bitter cold. We headed towards the Red Light District. Ah, Amsterdam, the Las Vegas of Europe. From the tram, we headed to the metro station to the 53 train to the Red Light District. In case you didn't know, and I would find hard to believe you didn't, prostitution is legal there and unionized. They have a health plan, dental plan, possibly a 401k retirement plan. When we got out of the metro station, we headed down the narrow walkways of the Red Light District. As I walked with Alejandra, she told me how it worked: "So when the light is on, there is a prostitute who is working. If the shades are shut on the door, she's working. If she's at the door, she's looking for customers."

"Interesting," I said.

As we walked through, Alejandra said, "What about that one? That one has nice tits. Let's try her."

I was getting beet red, and she was laughing at me because I was embarrassed. We headed to shops, and Alejandra went back and forth. Then I saw an oasis in this wintry abyss: a bar! "Honey, I'm going to hang out there while you shop. Is that okay?" I pointed to the bar.

"Sure, knock yourself out," she said.

I walked into the bar and ordered an Amstel Light, nectar of the gods, one of my favorite beers of all time—and I was in the place where they brew it. Man, after that first taste . . . It was the freshest Amstel Light I had ever had. I looked around and saw a rugby game on the TV. I turned around and looked outside. There was an eight-foot gray thing with four sides in the middle of the square. I thought, *what the fuck is that monstrosity?* Then I saw a guy walk up to it and start pissing in it. Then another guy went to the right of him and did the same thing. It was an outdoor urinal! I laughed and thought, "Talk about shrinkage."

After a couple of beers, I asked the bartender, "Where's the restroom?"

The bartender pointed, and you guessed it: outside, that gray monstrosity.

I nodded my head and said, "I'll be right back," to the bartender so that he wouldn't close my tab.

I put my blue wool NY Yankees hat and winter coat on and headed to the outdoor urinal. I didn't put on my gloves because of sanitary reasons, and I proceeded to walk right up to the urinal to undo my fly and take out Mr. Happy. He was far from happy. It was negative two outside, and he had to come out of his warm pouch. I pissed and was surprised my piss didn't freeze on contact with the air. My dick shrunk up to the size of a cocktail weenie. Thank God Alejandra wasn't there, or she would probably have divorced me on the spot. I finished, ran inside, and asked for a shot of Jameson whiskey to warm me up. The bartender obliged and poured it, and I downed it and chased it with my beer.

I was now four Amstels and one shot of whiskey in and feeling really good about myself when Alejandra walked in. She saw the shit-eating grin on my face, laughed, and took a swig of my beer, and knew I was buzzed. "How we doing?" she asked.

"Fan-fucking-tastic," I said, giving her the okay sign with my right hand.

"How many have you had?" she asked.

"Don't know. Real men don't count," I said and laughed at my own joke.

"Let's go back to the hotel," she said.

"Okay, but I got to piss first," I said. And I put on my winter coat and wool hat and headed to the outdoor urinal.

Alejandra said, "Where are you going?"

I pointed to the outdoor urinal and ran to it to pee. Little did I know, Alejandra took a photo of me pissing at the urinal from behind.

I ran back into the bar and found her laughing. I closed out my tab, and we headed out the door into the biting cold. The cold gave me that shock and sobered me up a little. She took my hand, and we walked back through the Red Light District. As we were walking, I got an idea: if Alejandra pulled that "what about her, babe" shit again, I was going to surprise her.

Sure enough, there was a beautiful Spanish woman in the door wearing a black bikini. She had great tits and nice legs and ass. Alejandra said, "What about her?"

Put "Possible Threesome Plan" into effect. I didn't say anything. I grabbed Alejandra's hand and took the doorknob with my other hand as the Spanish prostitute watched.

Alejandra said, "What the fuck are you doing?"

"She's cute. Let's do it."

"Not in your life, mister," she yelled.

I laughed, and she pushed me. "You're drunk. I forgot: no inhibitions."

"Correct," I said. "Next time, don't tempt me."

She shook her head. "Men."

We headed back to the metro, took it to the tram, and walked about 300 yards to our hotel. We got into our room, and I attacked Alejandra—one, because I was horny, and two, because I was a little drunk. We proceeded to undress but still keep our long johns on because we were still thawing out from the cold. We got under the covers of our queen-size bed and held each other to warm up. We started kissing and making out and groping each other. Eventually, we took off the bottoms of each other's long johns. Alejandra hopped on my dick and started to ride. We had amazing sex—for body warmth purposes.

We woke up the next morning to snow and zero-degree temperatures. We asked the concierge where the locals eat breakfast, and he said there was a great breakfast place off the third tram stop to our right. We walked in the snow and wind to the tram and, luckily, we had to wait only two minutes for the tram to come. We entered into the blissful heat.

On the tram, I noticed every Dutch person was about six feet, four inches tall. Alejandra looked at me quizzically and asked, "What's up?"

"Everyone is huge! I'm five feet eleven inches, and I'm 25 percent Dutch."

"So, what happened?" she asked, laughing.

"I don't know. That's what I'm trying to figure out," I said, laughing back.

We got off at the stop and went to our concierge's suggested restaurant. It was packed. The hostess brought us upstairs to a table by the window. We ordered waffles and coffee. While making small talk, Alejandra and I looked outside, and the snow was now blowing diagonally, coming down in a squall. We saw a woman on a bicycle with her five-year-old in a wooden cart on the handlebars, riding through the streets like it was a seventy-five-degree sunny day.

"Are you seeing this?" I said.

"Yes," Alejandra said, shocked.

"Wow, that's impressive," I said.

"It is."

"The cold doesn't bother either of them. They are riding around like this is normal."

"This is normal to them, C. J."

"Right," I said. Check off European places I don't want to retire to. Too cold, although Amsterdam is a nice place to visit.

The squall stopped, and we paid the bill and hit the town. First, the Van Gogh Museum, which is magnificent (no ear though, in case you were wondering. You'd think that would be in a jar on display or something.) Then the Heineken Museum, which was incredible, by far the freshest Heineken I had ever tasted. Then the Anne Frank House.

As a Language Arts teacher and having read *The Diary of Anne Frank* with my students, it was incredibly moving and powerful to go through the false bookcase wall, up the narrow, six-inch, steep steps into the secret annex to see where the Frank family and the Van Daans lived and survived for that time. Seeing Anne Frank's room and the posters she put up there was so moving, I remembered the last line of her diary: "I keep my ideals, because in spite of everything, I still believe that people are really good at heart."

I had tears in my eyes when we left. Alejandra and I and everyone else who was in the house were so quiet and respectful, almost as if it was holy ground. To be truthful, it is.

That night, Alejandra and I took a canal ride through Amsterdam. Luckily, the boat was covered, so we were not exposed to the elements while on the Amstel River. We sat on one of the benches, and I turned to Alejandra and said, "This is where the beer comes from."

She laughed and said, "You're an idiot," and she wrapped her arm around mine to give me a kiss.

I laughed. "God, I love you."

"I love you, too."

After a half hour, our boat ride ended, and we had to find an internet cafe so that we could list for our flight back to the States. We asked around, and everyone told us, "We don't know of any internet cafes around here."

"Great, how can a concierge be wrong about her own city?" How the hell were we getting home if we couldn't get internet? It was 2009. Everyone couldn't be high and fucking all the time in Amsterdam, could they? We walked for a good twenty minutes and asked a waffle vendor parked outside the Space Cakes Marijuana/Coffee Bar ("Because when too much coffee leads me to become edgy, I can smoke a joint and kick back yet still have that caffeine rush"—Amsterdam's new slogan.)

Alejandra asked the waffle vendor, "Do you know where there is an internet cafe?"

"Yes." He pointed to Space Cakes.

"You got to be fucking kidding me," I said.

"Nope, that's the only one around here," he said.

"Great," I said sarcastically.

Alejandra said, "You have to go in there and log in and list us on tomorrow's flight."

"Why do I have to do it?" I asked.

"Because I get randomly drug tested, that's why," she exclaimed.

"You do know that I am a State employee, and I, too, get drug

ALONG FOR THE RIDE

tested?" I retorted.

"Yes, when you're first hired," she fired back.

She turned to the vendor. "Do you have a pen?"

He gave her a pen.

She wrote all the information on a napkin and said, "List us on a vacation pass and for first class."

"Yes, love."

I walked into Space Cakes and descended the five concrete steps into the Marijuana Bar. I opened the wooden door, and there was a six-and-a-half-foot, 270-pound, muscular man sitting to my right. He looked at me, and I looked at him and said, "Internet?"

"Yes, just pay him over there." He pointed to the guy behind the marijuana bar; I guess he would be called the marijuana bartender. Let's call him Mary Jane. I walked over to him, and behind glass were all different kinds of marijuana. Truth be told, in college I smoked some marijuana, but I wouldn't know the difference from one type or the other or even the difference in buzz content.

I asked him, "Internet?"

"Yes, ten euros," said Mary Jane.

I paid him the ten euros, and he gave me the login name and password for computer number 5, which was on the back wall between two hoople heads who were getting high as a kite. Fantastic.

I sat at computer 5 and entered the login code and password. Computer 4 hoople head was smoking through a bong and blowing it freely in my direction. Computer 6 hoople head was rolling a joint, lighting it up, and asking me through hand gestures if I would like to partake. I shook my head and held my right hand up, giving him the universal no signal.

I logged into the computer, and the contact high was starting to happen. Because of it, I was messing up the login for Alejandra's Global Airlines website. I was concentrating yet still fucking up because the smoke from computer 4 kept flowing in my direction. Did anyone have a fan? I finally got logged in and listed us for the first flight to Newark that left at 9:30 a.m., first class. I printed out the boarding passes, logged out, walked over to Mary Jane, and collected my boarding passes at the printer beside him. I noticed that I had no pain in my knees or back. I was feeling really relaxed. *Oh shit, I'm high.*

I got my passes, said goodbye to Mary Jane, and walked past the bouncer and up the steps to Alejandra.

"You were in there for a while, what happened?"

"How long was I gone?" I asked.

"Fifteen minutes," she said.

I told Alejandra the whole story, and she looked at me and saw that my eyes were glassy. "You're high, aren't you?"

"Yes, but it's a contact high. I did not inhale, to quote President Clinton."

She laughed.

"I'm hungry. Do you want to get a waffle?"

9

Christmas at the Airport

ON CHRISTMAS EVE IN 2009, I came home from dropping off some gifts at a family friend's house to find my wife crying hysterically on the couch in the living room. I immediately ran to her and asked her, "What happened? Are you okay? Did someone die?"

"No, I'm just sad," she said through sobs.

"Why are you sad? This is one of the happiest times on the planet. It's Christmastime. Our son, Jack, is healthy and happy. What's going on?"

"I haven't been home for Christmas in seven years, and now it's going to be eight tomorrow!" She started crying again.

"Alejandra, have you checked any flights?"

"Yes, they are all full. Everything is oversold," she said sadly.

"Can I check and see?"

I logged in to the Global Airlines website and checked flights from Newark to Houston, and Newark to Denver. Everything was oversold by twenty. I went to Custom Routing, where I could pick the airport and figure out how many stops I could get to the next airport. I went through my mental Rolodex of NFL Teams, because I'm a huge football fan and this is how I breakdown the country. To go west, we needed to figure out connections from here to somewhere to get to El Paso, Texas.

A normal trip to El Paso, Texas, is an eight-hour affair if the planets line up right and you make the connecting flight. I started with the NFC East since I'm a diehard New York Giants fan, then checked Philadelphia. Nope. Oversold by fifteen to Houston. DC, oversold by twelve. I worked over to the NFC North: Chicago—no chance in hell! Minnesota, nope! Green Bay, they don't even fly to Detroit—no connection. I went through every division in the National Football Conference and no dice! I headed over to the AFC East then the AFC North: Pittsburgh! There were three seats on the 9 a.m. flight to Pittsburgh! Now to get south. The flight to Pittsburgh was two hours and landed at 11:10 a.m. Now, here was the rub: I had to find empty flights from 11:30 a.m. onto somewhere in the Southwest region of the country. From there, an eight- to ten-hour car ride was doable. I looked at Pittsburgh to Houston: ten seats on the 4:30 p.m. flight landing in Houston at 7:40. I needed one more flight to make it work. Fingers crossed, I typed in Houston to El Paso at 9:30 p.m. I clicked on the flight totals: five seats available! That's it! I got the flight plan we would take to El Paso on Christmas Day! The 9:30 p.m. flight landed at 11 p.m. mountain time.

I told Alejandra, "I got it. Newark to Pittsburgh, Pittsburgh to Houston, Houston to El Paso."

"What? Let me see that." Alejandra looked at the laptop and said, "A lot of things have to break right for this to happen. I'm not sure."

"I promise you, I will get you to El Paso tomorrow on Christmas," I said.

"Okay, let's try," she said in a quiet voice and gave me a long kiss.

"Go get packed," I told her.

We listed ourselves and Jack for the flight. Since Jack was a four-month-old, he'd be a lap child. We packed until midnight. I put the luggage in the car and went to bed. Alejandra put her arm on my chest and said, "Thank you, and I love you for trying to make this happen. And even if it doesn't, I love you even more because you tried to do this for me." She kissed me gently.

"I love you too, and Merry Christmas." I slipped my right hand under her pajama bottoms to grab her ass, then proceed to move her on top of me for some serious bumping and grinding.

We shed our pajamas and fucked passionately. In the six years I'd been with Alejandra, I think we'd made love about two times. We fuck! We don't make love. It was wild and animalistic, just how God intended sex to be. All positions all the time!

We woke up, got ready, and headed to the airport. Alejandra checked the flights. Newark to Pittsburgh was now negative one. Alejandra said, "I don't think we're going to make it. Pittsburgh is negative one, and there's nothing getting out of Newark."

"How do the connecting flights look?" I asked

"They're open, if we get to Pittsburgh," she said.

"Let's try. Worse-case scenario, we head back home," I said.

We got to the airport, parked in the employee lot, took the employee bus to the airport, got through security, and waited at the gate. The airport was mobbed, and I stayed with Jack in our chair as Alejandra headed towards the gate agent, a slim, white woman who looked flustered behind the podium and was staring at the computer screen.

I saw Alejandra and the woman behind the counter make small talk, and I could tell Alejandra had become friends with her. She headed back to us and said, "It's now at zero. There is a chance we may get on the flight. We're the first three on the non-rev list."

"Okay, it looked like you were becoming friends over there," I said.

"Her name is Danielle. She is very friendly and overwhelmed, and I asked her if she wanted help, since I work for Global. She appreciated it, and we just hit it off," she stated.

"You're amazing. I envy you that you have that ability to make friends instantly," I said.

They started boarding, and Alejandra and I prayed we would all get on. With ten minutes left to wheels up, Danielle started calling names from the non-rev list: "Nicholas party of three!"

Alejandra ran to Danielle. "We're right here," she said.

"I've got two seats. You're not together, but you're on. The baby will be on your lap," Danielle stated.

Alejandra started crying (tears of joy this time). "Thank you, Danielle! You're my Christmas angel. God bless you!"

"Merry Christmas. Get on the flight," she said.

We boarded the flight, and Alejandra asked the man sitting next to me, "Could I sit next to my husband? I have an aisle seat, and here's a free drink ticket if you do."

The man complied, and the door closed. We were on our way to Pittsburgh. The flight was uneventful until the descent. It had snowed in Western Pennsylvania on Christmas Eve, and we could see the snow on the ground from the air. As the plane was descending, it hit air pockets and wind. We were violently dropping six to ten feet per second and grabbing both seat handles because there isn't that oh-shit handle like they have on the passenger side of cars. My stomach was fluttering because my insides were going up and down from the turbulence.

"Jesus Christ," I said to Alejandra.

"Babe, relax. If we go down, at least we die as a family," she said in a comforting tone, "like *The Notebook*."

"We really need to work on your timing and bedside manner," I said.

We landed with a loud thud and thankfully in one piece. We taxied to the gate, got out of our seats, collected Jack's stroller at the bottom of the jetway, and headed to the arrival/departure board to see which gate the Pittsburgh-to-Houston flight was at.

"Gate 73," I said.

"We've got a lot of time to kill," Alejandra said. "Let's change Jack and then walk around the airport."

We changed Jack, then looked at the shops in the Pittsburgh airport. While shopping, I noticed that the airport was relatively empty, unlike Newark at noon on Christmas Day. I walked past an Irish bar that was empty but open, and right across from it by the escalators was a colorful sculpture of Franco Harris for his famous catch of "The Immaculate Reception." It showed him bent over, catching a football by his feet, resulting in the Pittsburgh Steelers first trip to the Super Bowl. I took a photo and sent it to my diehard Steeler fan friend, George, with a text saying, "Merry Christmas from Pittsburgh!"

Alejandra and Jack came from a store, and I asked Alejandra, "Why don't we eat Christmas Dinner at this Irish Pub, considering we are not going to have a chance later due to our connections?"

"Okay," Alejandra said.

We entered the empty restaurant, sat at a table, and each ordered a burger and a beer. I toasted with my wife: "To making it to El Paso today and a safe journey and Merry Christmas."

"Merry Christmas and amen," she said.

"Cheers," I said.

"Cheers," she said back. We clinked glasses and drank our beers.

We ate and made small talk. After finishing our dinner, we left the waitress a Christmas tip (she was working on a holiday when she should have been home with her family, but we were thankful that she was, so that we could eat our Christmas dinner as a family on our way to see the rest of our family). We headed to the gate and found an elderly couple berating the gate agent.

The woman, who was in a wheelchair, was yelling, "You better sit my husband next to me, or it'll be your job! I am the customer, and I am always right!"

I thought, *what an asshole.* We sat in the chairs by the gate, and the woman would not shut up, continuing to berate him. "Give me your supervisor's number. I'll call Global Airlines myself and tell them what an awful job you're doing!"

The gate agent, Greg, was an African-American who was wearing glasses and doing his best to stay calm rather than angry at his customer, even though she was being impossible. He started the boarding process, calling for people with small children, military personnel, or people who needed help down the jetway to board first.

The woman went first with her husband and got separate tickets from the gate agent. She continued to berate him down the jetway. "How dare you separate us! I'm going to have your job!"

He called, "Nicholas party of three."

We ran to him and received our tickets. He said, "I put you guys together because of the baby."

"Thank you," I said. "We really appreciate that, and I'm sorry you're taking shit from that woman."

"Don't worry about it. I'd rather help people who are respectful than that woman. Enjoy your flight," Greg said.

We walked down the jetway, dropped our stroller off at the bottom, and boarded the plane. The woman in the wheelchair was still yelling about being separated from her husband, now directing her wrath on the flight attendants. "This airline is shit. I'm calling all your supervisors, and I will have all your jobs tomorrow!"

We sat down, and Greg boarded to check the seat count. The old woman saw him and started in on him: "You did this to us on purpose to accommodate that family!" She pointed to us. "How dare you split up my husband and I!"

"That's it," Greg yelled. "I've been working here for fifteen years, and you are by far the worst customer I have ever encountered. I have been patient, and now I'm done." He turned to the lead flight attendant. "Call the captain!"

The lead flight attendant called the captain, who walked out of the cockpit, a six-feet-four-inches, 250-pound muscular gentleman with salt and pepper hair. "What's going on?" he asked.

Greg told him the whole story. The woman tried interrupting Greg, but the captain said, "Ma'am, I need to listen."

She said, "I'm the customer! You should be listening to me! What is wrong with you people!"

The captain stopped Greg and turned to the elderly passenger. "Ma'am, let me say this so we are clear. You have proven Greg here to be correct in his argument, so I am going to give you two choices: A, you leave now in handcuffs from the air marshals, and they will throw you in jail on Christmas Day because you are unruly, or B, you sit there and don't say another word. If during the flight, I find out you so much as raised your voice to anyone in this cabin, I will have you arrested by the air marshals in Houston. Do you understand me?"

She immediately shut up. The captain turned around, and the entire cabin erupted in applause.

The rest of the flight was uneventful. The elderly woman said nothing to anyone on the flight, and we reached Houston on time. We deplaned and looked at the arrival/departure board.

"El Paso 9:30 p.m. flight is on time and departing at Concourse 3." Alejandra, Jack, and I got the stroller, strapped Jack in it, and headed for Concourse 3. We started running to the monorail. Since the monorail is above the concourse, we had to take an elevator because of the stroller. We got off the elevator and waited for the monorail. A minute and thirty seconds later, we got on the monorail and took two stops to Concourse 3. We exited, ran to the elevator, and pressed the button. It opened, and I hit the down button and waited for the doors to open.

They opened, and we ran to our gate. Concourse 3 was a long, snakelike terminal. We arrived at Gate 96, and Alejandra approached the gate agent, showed her Global Airlines credentials, and asked about standbys.

Gina, the gate agent, said, "You're getting on," and smiled as she printed out our boarding passes.

"Thank you so much, and Merry Christmas," Alejandra said cheerfully.

"We're going to El Paso," she told me with a kiss. "I love you."

"I love you, too," I said.

We boarded the plane to El Paso and literally slept the entire flight. Jack had been perfect the entire day. With a half hour left in the flight, the flight attendant announced, "We are making our descent into El Paso, please return your seats and tray tables to their full and upright positions."

It was 11:30 p.m. mountain time when we landed in El Paso. We had been traveling for fifteen hours, through four different airports; we'd eaten Christmas dinner in an Irish airport pub in Pittsburgh; and we were thoroughly jetlagged and exhausted.

But as the old Mastercard commercials used to say, "Seeing the beaming smile on my wife's face, priceless!"

"Merry Christmas, baby," I whispered in her ear, not wanting to wake Jack.

"Merry Christmas, love," she said.

Promise kept and with a half hour to spare.

10

Rome

"BABE, FOR MY FORTIETH BIRTHDAY, I want a big party with all my friends and family at a hall so we can celebrate. We can have it catered, get a DJ, get some booze, hire a bartender. It will be great. What do you think?" Alejandra asked.

"Sure, if that's what you want," I replied.

It was January, so I had six months to prepare. I asked the local firehouse up the street about their catering hall. The price was reasonable, so I put a hundred-dollar deposit down to reserve the date in July. I had a month to get my money back for free cancellation.

Flashforward to February: Alejandra came home one day from work and said, "I don't want a party now for my birthday. I want to go to Italy and the Amalfi Coast."

"I just put down a deposit two weeks ago for the hall," I retorted. "Why did you change your mind?"

"I was thinking, as much as I want a party, I would much rather go on a trip with you," she says.

"What about the kids?" I asked.

We now had two children: Jack was four, and Sophia was two.

"We'll take them to El Paso, and my mother and sister can watch them," she said.

"How long are we going for?"

"Ten days."

"And your mom and sister are cool with this?" I asked.

"I haven't asked them yet, but I think they would do it," Alejandra said.

"You may want to ask them before you book this trip and I ask for my deposit back from the fire department."

"Don't worry. I will ask them," Alejandra said.

A week later, Alejandra confirmed with both her mom and sister that they would watch our kids. We just had to fly them down to El Paso, and they would take care of the rest.

I went up the street and asked for my deposit back from the fire department, stating the reason why as, "We wanted to go in a different direction." I wanted to let them down gently.

Alejandra planned to fly into Rome from Newark and spend four days there. We would then take a train to the Amalfi Coast and spend six days in Positano at a bed and breakfast. The total time we were away from home was almost a month—a week in El Paso to drop off the kids and see family, ten days in Italy, another five days in El Paso to pick up the kids and see family again, and two days in Minneapolis so I could graduate with my master's degree from Capella University.

We flew the kids to El Paso, had no problems making the flight or our connections, and had a great time seeing friends. The night before we were supposed to leave for Rome, Italy, Alejandra called a cab to arrive at my mother-in-law's house at 4:30 a.m. so we could take the 6:00 a.m. flight to Houston to connect to Newark and from Newark to Italy. Basically, we would be spending the entire day in the air or an airport.

We packed the night before and kissed Jack and Sophia good night. Alejandra informed me that we were not going to make the Newark to Rome flight because it was oversold. She did some searching and said, "We can make it to DC, and Dulles leaves for Rome at the same time as Newark."

"Okay, you're the boss," I said.

The alarm rang at 4 a.m., and we were dressed and ready to go with luggage outside the house, awaiting the cab for the 4:30 pick-up. These were the pre-Uber days. While we were waiting, Alejandra started crying—bawling.

"What's the matter?" I asked.

"I can't do it. I can't leave my babies," Alejandra said through tears.

"Well, you knew we were going to do this, six months ago, when you came up with this idea. Do you want to cancel the trip?" I asked.

"No, I can do this," she said through sobs.

"We can go to the Inn of the Mountain Gods for the weekend, if you want," I said. The Inn at the Mountain Gods is a beautiful hotel and casino in Ruidoso, New Mexico, kind of like Atlantic City Light.

"No, I can do this. I just had to get this out of my system," Alejandra said.

"Okay."

The orange cab pulled down the street and turned into the driveway. "Last chance," I said.

"We're going," she replied.

I helped the cabbie load our luggage into the trunk and made sure he took everything.

"The airport," I said.

We rode to the airport, and Alejandra leaned into my chest, looked up at me, said, "Thank you," and kissed me.

We arrived at El Paso International Airport and checked our bags to Washington, DC. When we arrived in DC, we had to exit security, re-check our bags to Rome, and go through security at Dulles Airport. Ah, the joys of non-revving. Luckily, we had time to do this since our flight arrived at 3 p.m. and the next one left at 7 p.m. for Rome. We had two hours to kill and decided to go down and have dinner.

"Let's call my mom," Alejandra said.

She called her mom and talked to the kids.

"They're fine, *mija*," her mom said. "Have a great time. We'll Facetime when you reach Italy on Sunday," she said.

"Are the kids okay?" I asked.

"Yes, fine," Alejandra said.

"Are you okay with leaving the kids with your family?"

"Yes, I'm fine. I just needed to get it out this morning," she said.

We made the flight and sat in coach. The flight was uneventful, which is great. I slept through the whole flight—three vodkas and Sprites will do that to you (thank you, alcohol). Alejandra woke me up and pushed the window shade up as we touched down on Italian soil on a beautiful sunny morning.

I smiled. "We're here."

"Yep." Alejandra smiled back.

We exited the plane, went to baggage claim, got our bags, and caught a train from the metro station to our hotel. We were two blocks away from the Coliseum. We got off the metro and were hit by stifling heat and humidity. It was ninety-seven degrees with 100 percent humidity—great weather if you're from Mercury. At the end of our two-block hotel trek, I was dripping with sweat. It looked as if I'd run a marathon. August in Italy—it's a scorcher!

We opened the door to our two-star hotel and met with the concierge, Piero, who directed us to our room, which we were allowed to check-in to immediately. We entered our second-floor room. It was a decent size, but there was a piece of ceiling tile on the bed. Apparently, someone was having wild sex above us. Good for them, but that's a pretty large fucking ceiling tile. We asked Piero for a different room, and he obliged, offering us the next room over. The room was the same minus the ceiling tile. We said, *grazie* and *ciao* to Piero and showered. After our shower, we napped to adjust to the time change and woke up at 4 p.m. Rome time.

We got dressed and went downstairs to ask Piero how far the Coliseum was from here. He gave us a map and said in broken English and a thick Italian accent, "Stay left at the fork in the road, and you will run into it."

"*Grazie*, Piero," Alejandra said.

"*Prego.*"

We left "Hotel Falling Ceiling Tile" and followed the map, heading toward the Coliseum. The sun was setting, and we were walking on the cobblestone streets of Rome hand in hand. Rome was beautiful. We stayed left at the fork in the road, and there it was—amazing!

We crossed the busy street and walked around it. Visiting hours were over, but we were taking photos of the outside of it. It was now nightfall, and we decided to go to a restaurant for dinner and ate right across the street from the Coliseum, where they used to keep the animals (tigers and lions) and parade them under the road into the stadium. It's amazing that the holding pen is still there.

After dinner, we headed across the street, took a couple of

more photos, and walked back to "Hotel Falling Ceiling Tile." We entered the room, and I was all over Alejandra. She wanted to sleep, but I wanted to fuck and then sleep. You see, if you fuck first, you get tired, and sleep is easier for both people. Plus, I had a rule: since we were in a different country or city, we had to have sex in it. Guys, try this with your girlfriends or wives: "Honey, when is the next time we'll be in Rome? Might as well enjoy it and each other?" It's worked for me.

Alejandra caved, and we had great sex. I wonder if we knocked off any ceiling tile on the first floor?

Our four days in Rome were a whirlwind. We spent a day at the Vatican, because we are Catholic. It was amazing, and we saw all the sights, including the guy blowing wind on the ground where they shot the movie *Angels and Demons*.

Piero told us, "Go to the Vatican in the afternoon to avoid the lines; it is less crowded."

"*Grazie*, Piero," Alejandra said.

We took his advice and went in the afternoon. We headed on the metro and had a three-block walk to Vatican City. We made the walk, but it was hot! We were sweating; it was so damn humid. We brought water bottles with us, and all throughout Rome they had water fountains. Thank God they do, because we were going through water like no tomorrow, refilling the bottles, putting the water on the backs of our necks and face. I was practically bathing in it; it was that hot.

We entered St. Peter's Basilica. It was enormous. There were no lines to get into the Vatican, unlike the water fountains, which were six-people deep in a cue. We walked through security and the metal detectors and into the Vatican Museum to see the Sistine Chapel. The museum is a labyrinth of twists and turns, and on the way, there are paintings and sculptures. Yes, some nude sculptures as well. I leaned into Alejandra's ear. "Are we getting horny?" I hoped and prayed the answer was yes.

"What gave you that idea?" she asked.

"Nude sculptures."

"I might be," she said matter-of-factly.

"I can arrange something later."

She leaned into my ear and said, "You better."

We eventually got into the Sistine Chapel. There were no pictures or talking allowed in the chapel. The only talking is people whispering and a person on a recording saying on an amplifier, "Silence, please!" in several different languages. How Michelangelo did this, God only knows, because it is beautiful and really high off the ground.

From there we went to the Basilica. It was the most incredible church I had ever seen. If you don't believe in God after leaving the Vatican, then you're truly an atheist.

The next three days, we visited the Spanish Steps, the Trevi Fountain, the Coliseum, the Forum, Piazza Novona, and the Castile San Angelo.

On our way out of Castile San Angelo, Alejandra pulled out her planner and her Frommer's *Italy Guide Book*. We were standing on the *ponte* (Italian for bridge), and she was trying to get her bearings.

"What are you doing?" I asked.

"I'm trying to figure out where the road is for this convent," she replied.

"We're going to a convent?"

"Yes, for lunch," she said.

"Why a convent? Aren't there restaurants around here? Do the Sisters of Perpetual Motion own a restaurant?"

"One of my colleagues gave me an address of a convent

around here and says they serve the best lunch that you will have in Rome. It's not touristy, and it's cheap," she said.

"Okay, lead the way."

Alejandra looked at her guidebook, and the map told her that we had to cross the bridge and the very busy road, then go down a set of steps to a side street running diagonally from the Castile San Angelo. We followed the directions and looked for ten minutes without finding it. Nothing looked like a convent. We finally found the exact address; it looked nothing like a convent and more like a three-story apartment building.

"This is the address, but does this look like a convent to you?" I asked.

"No, but let's ring the bell and find out."

We rang the bell, and a woman answered the door. She was a middle-aged woman wearing a dress, no habit. Alejandra asked, "*Scusi, Signora, è questo il convento?*" ("Excuse me, ma'am, is this the convent?" Yes, Alejandra is fluent in Italian too.)

"*Sì,*" she said, and allowed us to enter.

We were led through a room and down a set of steps to the basement of the convent where locals were eating lunch.

We sat at a table for two and spoke to a nun in English. She asked us, "How did you know about us?"

"My friend gave us this address and said it was the best meal in Rome," Alejandra replied.

"Your friend is right," the sister said.

She brought us water and a loaf of bread (Italian bread, of course).

"You'd think they would put a sign up, or a cross, or a crucifix, to let people know this is the building," I said.

"You're right," Alejandra replied.

The nun, let's call her Sister Isabella, came back with two

different types of pasta: penne in marinara and bowties in pesto. We scooped both pastas out on to our plates. A minute later, Sister Isabella came back with a chicken dish and put two pieces of grilled chicken on our plates. This convent was one of those Arthur Avenue Restaurant types in the Bronx, New York, where there are no menus. It's just what they feel like cooking that day.

"*Grazie*," we said.

"*Prego*," Sister Isabella replied.

The food was delicious, and we finished all of it. Then Sister Isabella came out with a fruit plate. We had grapes and finally finished our meal. The bill came out to ten euros each.

"Sister, you're kidding. Twenty euros?" I said.

"Is that too much?" she asked.

"No, it's too little. That meal was a four-course lunch. In New York City, I would have paid two hundred!" I said.

She laughed, and I handed her twenty euros and gave her ten euros as a tip. She said, "What's this for?"

"A tip, Sister."

"I can't take this. We take an oath of poverty," Sister Isabella said.

"Sister, can you take a donation?" I asked.

"Yes, but to whom?" she asked.

"Any charity you see fit."

"Bless you."

"*Grazie*, Sister."

Remember, scoring points with God is always good. This is today's public service announcement.

Alejandra and I were stuffed and glad for the long walk to "Hotel Falling Ceiling Tile."

"That was the best meal I've had in Rome," I told Alejandra. "Tell your friend that was an excellent spot and thank her for me."

"Oh my God, yes, that was so worth it!"

"Where to now?" I asked.

"Some shopping," she said.

Yay. Jazz Hands. I would rather run face first into a brick wall at full speed, get up, and do it again than shop.

"I want to get you some ties," Alejandra said.

"Okay," I said reluctantly. "Can I tie you up in them later?"

She laughed. "If you're lucky and don't give me a hard time."

I sat in a chair and watched Alejandra in all her glory. Even if she was shopping for me, I was bored. I picked two silk, Italian ties: a light-green striped tie, and a yellow-and-blue striped tie. Alejandra bought some clothes, and we finally left the store. I was on my best behavior as we took the metro to "Hotel Falling Ceiling Tile."

"Do you want dinner?" I asked.

"No, I'm still full, but I'll tell you what I do want."

"What's that?"

"To shower and try out your new ties."

"Yes, ma'am." Inside, I was weeping with joy.

We entered "Hotel Falling Ceiling Tile," said *ciao* to Piero (didn't that guy get a day off?), got into our room, stripped, and attacked each other in the shower. We washed each other thoroughly, dried off, and continued where we'd left off, using my ties quite effectively.

God, I love Italy.

11

Amalfi Coast

THE FOLLOWING DAY, WE CHECKED out of "Hotel Falling Ceiling Tile" and took two trains and a bus to the Amalfi Coast, more specifically Positano, Italy. The trains were not the luxury bullet trains. Ours were circa 1970s *The Warriors* movie trains with graffiti all over them, no air conditioning, and all windows down because it was ninety-seven degrees and 100 percent humidity in a steel car.

We met some fellow Americans on the train and made small talk. "Where are you going?" asked Alejandra to the long-haired brunette named Laura. She was in her mid-thirties.

"Sorrento, then Capri," she said.

"Capri, wow. We're going to visit for the day while we're in Positano," Alejandra replied.

"A friend told us they saw Steven Tyler last week in Capri," Laura said.

"Nice," I said.

We got off at Sorrento, said goodbye to Laura and her friends, and checked the bus schedule to get to Positano. The bus we were directed to departed at 12:30 p.m. and arrived around 1 p.m. in Positano. The bus was smaller than most American buses, about eight feet wide and fourteen feet long, but it was heaven sent—air-conditioned.

On a personal note, the SITA bus drivers are the best in the world. Why? They drive a bus on a windy narrow road, leaving no room for error. If the bus driver makes a mistake, you either hit a brick wall or fall 300 feet to your death into the Tyrrhenian Sea. Everyone else driving on the Amalfi Coast uses a Smart Car.

As Alejandra and I were sitting and enjoying the air conditioning, we enjoyed the most beautiful scenery: deep blue water and pastel houses and apartments. At 1 p.m., we reached our stop at the top of Positano overlooking a breathtaking view of the beach below. We had three roller boards with us. Alejandra asked a store owner where Villa Gemma was located.

The woman answered, "*Segui la strada, sali e non scendi e vedrai un cartello.*" ("Follow the road, go up not down, and you will see a sign for it.")

"*Grazie*," Alejandra said.

The woman came outside, took Alejandra by the hand, and pointed to the villa. From my estimation, it was three levels higher than we were standing. Positano was built on the side of a cliff and shaped like a pyramid. We followed the road, and the sweat was pouring off me. I pushed a huge green suitcase and a purple flower roller board and carried my red backpack on my back, while Alejandra pushed a light-blue suitcase.

We walked for fifteen minutes and finally arrived at the villa. I was exhausted and needed a water break, air conditioning, and a chair. I looked at the entrance, which was a narrow passageway surrounded by vegetation on both sides. I took my suitcases through the gate. Oh, great: stairs. I turned to Alejandra. "Collapse your roller board. I'll bring the luggage up. You go ahead and find the owner."

"Good idea," she replied and collapsed her roller board.

I took the luggage up two flights of stairs, making three trips because the stairway was narrow and the bags weighed forty pounds each. I finally reached the top for the third and final time and met a salt-and-pepper-haired gentleman named Giovanni, who was the caretaker of the villa. He was dressed in khaki pants and a blue denim, long-sleeved button down. He didn't even seem to be sweating. I, on the other hand, looked as if I had finished a triathlon, and I could barely speak because I need water so badly.

"*Un momento por favore*," I said to Giovanni in broken Italian and a mouth like I'd just left the Sahara.

"*Certamente*," Giovanni said.

I grabbed the side of my red backpack where my water bottle was and took a long pull on it. I finished and put my hand out to Giovanni. "*Mi chiamo* C. J."

"I speak English," Giovanni said.

"Oh, thank God."

He laughed. "Your wife, Alejandra, took care of the check in. Let me take you to your room."

I took the big green bag and headed up another flight of stairs. It just wasn't my day for stairs. This would definitely qualify as leg day at the gym. I went back downstairs for the light-blue and purple flowered suitcases and brought them up. We walked through a white tiled hallway. At the end on the right hand side was our room. Giovanni opened the door with the key and showed us inside. It was huge (like seventy-five feet long and thirty feet wide) and stifling hot—about a hundred degrees! Our bed was a king with a sheet and no blanket. Alejandra opened the pocket door and walked out on the balcony. "Babe, come outside."

I walked outside and saw the most beautiful view of the entire town of Positano and the Tyrrhenian Sea below us. "Wow, what a view!" I said.

"I know, right," Alejandra said.

We turned around and Giovanni said, "You like?"

"Very much," we replied.

"One question, Giovanni: do you have air conditioning?" I asked.

"No air conditioning, just fans," he said.

No air conditioning? It was a billion degrees outside and humid, and they just had fans? That was like handling nuclear waste with an oven mitt. No good! Giovanni handed me the keys. I gave him a tip and checked the rest of the room. I passed the master bedroom as I walked farther in the hallway and to another door. I opened it and found another room with twin beds. I went back to the master bedroom suite, and on my right was the bathroom. I went in and spotted a window looking directly out from the shower. Oh, and there was a rooftop party going on at the hotel, and people were waving to me. I waved back, thinking people were going to get more of a show than they expected. I laughed to myself.

I took off my shirt; I was dripping with sweat. I turned on the ceiling fan and the two oscillating fans on each of the end tables of the beds. "God, it is so fucking hot," I said. "I'm going to shower."

"Okay, babe. I'll take one after you, and then we can go to dinner," Alejandra replied.

"Why don't you join me, and we can save the environment together," I said, hoping she'd take me up on it.

"It's too hot to fuck right now."

"Hence why I brought up the shower. You see, we can control the temperature and stay cool while we have some fun," I explained.

"Nice try, but no."

"Damn it, we can't have nice things."

She laughed, and I showered alone, disappointed. The cold water was fantastic and refreshing. I was doing my thing and happened to look out the window to find a couple of women looking at me from a higher diagonal view. They were waving and clapping. I saw what they were looking at: a perfect view of me and Mr. Happy. I blushed. But hey, when in Rome—or Positano. I turned and showed them my backside to more applause. Apparently, they liked what they saw, and now everyone in Italy knew that I was a whore for applause.

I finished showering, said goodbye to the ladies via wave, and toweled off. Alejandra came in and asked what was going on.

I showed her the window and said, "I was just putting on a show for those women." I waved to them, and they waved back.

Alejandra looked back, laughed, and waved. "Did they see your dick?"

"Yes, everything. It was a little bit embarrassing and titillating at the same time," I replied.

"You're a slut," she said, laughing.

"I try. If you'd come in and joined me, we really would have given them a show."

"I'm sure," she said. "How am I supposed to shower now?"

"You turn the knobs to the temperature you want and lift that thing on the faucet for the water to come out of the top," I said.

"No, you jerk. I'm sure people will be watching me now!"

"Yep, probably a slew of guys, and I can't blame them."

"I'll wait a half an hour."

"Okay, suit yourself," I said

Alejandra waited twenty minutes, looked out the window, found no one looking, and showered. She got out of the shower, and we changed for dinner.

We left our villa and saw Giovanni, and Alejandra asked him where the locals eat.

Giovanni said, "The tourists eat by the shore, and it is more expensive because you are closer to the water. But if you want the same meal for less of a price, go up a couple of streets to any of the restaurants. They are all good and cheaper."

"*Grazie*," Alejandra said.

"*Prego*," Giovanni retorted.

We left "Villa Sauna" and turned left to head up the road to a restaurant. After what seemed like two blocks (or two levels of the pyramid), we found a restaurant that seemed affordable. In those ten minutes, I was drenched in sweat. So much for the shower. We sat outside and had a beautiful view of the Tyrrhenian Sea. The waitress came up to us, a woman in her thirties, brown hair, brown eyes, full figured, huge tits, named Amara. We ordered pasta dishes with seafood, and it was incredible. We finished and the waitress asked if we'd like dessert.

"No, thank you," Alejandra said.

The waitress came back to our table with two shots of a yellow substance.

"What's that?" I asked. "We wanted the check," I said, laughing.

She said, "This is complementary. It's called limoncello."

"When in Rome, or Positano," I said.

"*Grazie*," we said and banged the shot back.

"That was delicious," I said.

The waitress said, "You're in the lemon-growing capital of the world."

"I did not know that," I replied.

She came back with two lemons the size of kiddie footballs. "Holy shit, those things are huge," I said, not referring to the waitresses' tits, even though she was holding the lemons at breast level.

"I told you," Amara said. "Here, hold one of them," she said to both of us.

She was talking about the lemons, right?

We each grabbed a lemon. It took two hands to hold it. Amara took a photo of us holding them before we handed them back.

I paid the bill, and we walked back to "Villa Sauna." On our walk back, we saw a set of steps with metallic railing on both sides. We decided to investigate. On further review, it was a steep set of concrete steps on a forty-five-degree angle, leading to the beach. Now I knew why there were handrails on both sides: if you fell, you were on a long, bumpy, and painful ride down to the beach. Alejandra said, "Let's check it out."

"Lead the way."

It took us five minutes to get to the bottom. I was again dripping in sweat. We went to our left and saw all the umbrellas ready for tomorrow's sun bathers. We passed a couple of booths saying "Trips to Capri."

"Well, now we know where to go for trips to Capri," Alejandra said.

"We'll ask them tomorrow, while we're here at the beach," I said.

We continued to walk along the shoreline and noticed a nightclub, La Terrazza dei Leoni, where there was live music and people enjoying themselves by eating and drinking and making merry. We looked at the menu, and Giovanni was right: the price of an entree was ten euros more than we'd paid earlier.

We decided to walk up the snakelike roads and visit some of the shops that were still open. We entered a clothing shop, and Alejandra did her thing browsing. I looked around and saw photos of celebrities who'd been in this store. Most of the photos were 8x10 glossy headshots, except the one with Colin Gallagher. In a 4x6 color photo, he was sitting with an elderly woman having a coffee with her. I asked the woman behind the cash register, "Why is this picture different from all the other celebrities?"

"Oh, Colin," she laughed. "He has a special relationship with my grandmother, the original owner of the store. He would have an espresso every day at lunch with her. They became very close."

"That's awesome," I said.

"I'll tell you a funny story: One day he was late getting here, and Nonna thought she got stood up. It turned out he overslept, and when he got here, the place was locked. He made so much of a commotion, other shop owners called the police because they thought he was trying to break in. The police brought my Nonna over in a police car so she could open the store, and they had espresso. The situation went back to normal," she said.

I laughed. "Great story."

We left the garment store and headed back to "Villa Sauna." Our room was still stifling hot. We walked onto the balcony and noticed another couple out on their balcony, two women, a blonde and a brunette. I waved hello. They waved back. Alejandra and I looked out at Positano below us, and to our left we saw all the yachts anchored in the Tyrrhenian Sea, their sailors enjoying the nightlife of Positano. The little shuttle boats beached on the shoreline awaited to take them back when they were done. Our balcony was pitch black, and there were no outside lights on, though there were two plastic chairs to sit on and enjoy the view. We showered and went to bed naked, because it was ninety-seven degrees in our room.

I woke up the next morning to something tugging on Mr. Happy—this time it wasn't me doing it.

"Morning. Someone is horny," I said groggily.

"I want sex," Alejandra said.

"Who am I to deny you such pleasure?"

After we finished, we dressed to go to the beach. But first a cafe americano with latte. We grabbed our towels and suntan lotion and put them in Alejandra's straw beach bag. We said *"bon giorno"* to Giovanni, who was still wearing the same clothes from yesterday.

"Bon giorno," he replied.

Alejandra asked where we could get a cafe americano.

He said, "Two doors to the left."

"Grazie, Giovanni."

"Prego."

"Babe, I forgot my sun hat. It's in the room. Can you go get it?"

"Sure," I said and headed back to the room.

As I walked back, I passed our blonde and brunette neighbors from last night. They saw me and both laughed.

Okay, I said to myself, why are they laughing? I then realized that we'd probably woke them up that morning with all the moaning and groaning from earlier. I smiled, knowing I did a good job.

I came back with Alejandra's sunhat, and we headed to the breakfast for *pane* (bread) and coffee. We each got a pastry. I had a cafe americano with latte while Alejandra had a cappuccino. We finished our beverages and went down the steep steps to the beach.

Our five-minute descent ended with me again drenched through. We made the left at the bottom and headed toward the orange umbrellas. We passed the booths that would take you to Capri, and there was a woman in it. Alejandra said, "Let's find out about going to Capri."

"Okay," I replied.

We waited for five minutes and spoke to an English woman named Emily who was in her thirties. "For forty euros," she said, "the boat will take you to and from Capri. Four hours on the actual island of Capri, you'll see the blue, green, and white grottos from the boat. Take two dips into the Tyrrhenian Sea. So, bring your bathing suits. I suggest you buy lunch here, because everything in Capri is super expensive."

Alejandra looked at me, and I nodded and paid her forty euros. Alejandra asked her, "Is there a local beach around here?"

"Well, yes, there is. And since you booked with me, I'll tell you how to get there," she said. "Go up this brick walkway and take it for ten minutes. You will run into a beach with white umbrellas and beach chairs. There will be a gray restaurant in front. Ask for Enzo; he is the owner of the beach. Tell him Emily sent you, and you will pay ten euros each for the day."

"Okay," I said. "Thank you."

"You're welcome, and be here tomorrow at 8 a.m. The boat leaves at 8:20."

We followed Emily's directions and in ten minutes came upon a beach with white umbrellas and white beach chairs behind a gray restaurant. We walked into the restaurant, where everyone was wearing bathing suits. A woman asked us if we would like to see a menu.

"Not right now. We are looking for Enzo?" I said.

A five-foot, eight-inch, 180-pound man with bronze skin and long, salt and pepper hair turned and eyed both of us. "I'm Enzo," he said.

I extended my hand and shook his. "Emily from the Capri booth sent us, told us to see you when we got here. We would like to stay at your beach for the day," I explained.

"Absolutely, come this way."

We followed him to two beach chairs and umbrellas and paid him twenty euros. "Anything you need, let me know," he said.

"*Grazie*," we said.

"*Prego*," Enzo replied and walked away.

"What do you think?" Alejandra asked.

"How do you get to be the sole owner of a beach in paradise?" I answered.

She laughed. "Great question. It's awesome."

We popped the umbrellas up because the sun was so hot, and we put suntan lotion on our bodies. I told Alejandra I was going into the water and would be back. She grabbed me, kissed me, and said, "No staring at topless twenty-five-year-old model's tits."

"Damn it. I'll try, but it's not like I called them to follow me to Italy," I said, thinking I should have gotten their numbers in Cascais for this occasion.

I left my flip flops by the chair and started walking to the shoreline. Big mistake. The white sand was on fire, and my feet were about to combust. When I reached the shoreline, I walked the rocks that led to the water. They were on fire. I have never walked across hot coals before, but I think it feels something like that. I got to the water and dove in. My feet finally cool, I popped my head out of the water, which stung my eyes. I tasted the salt on my lips and looked down into a deep blue sea that I could see my feet in, not Caribbean Blue, but a deep blue. The water was like bath water, high seventies or low eighties. After five minutes, I headed back to Alejandra. On the way, I noticed that people left their flip flops by the shoreline so they didn't burn their feet. Good tip. I'd do that when I went back in.

I got to our umbrellas and chairs and toweled off. "Any hot twenty-five-year-old topless models in the water with you?" Alejandra asked.

"Unfortunately, no. I'm quite disappointed. Not one topless person on this beach."

"It's still early yet," Alejandra said.

"Any chance of you doing that?" I asked, hoping to get a free show.

"No," she said sternly.

"Damn it."

We were sunbathing when we saw a man carrying an ice cream cooler and shouting, "Fresh coconut! It's the Coconut Man! Fresh coconut, one euro!"

"Coconut? That's refreshing on a hot day?" I asked Alejandra.

"Apparently—do you want to try some?" she said.

"Sure, why not."

I called the "Coconut Man" over and purchased two pieces of coconut. "Enjoy," I said. It was like eating bark—so dry that I literally spit it out. "That's disgusting," I said.

"Why don't you like it?" Alejandra asked.

"It's dry. That's refreshing? I think he should be sued for false advertising."

She laughed and enjoyed her bark.

We spend the day sunbathing, laughing, and swimming— although Alejandra only went calf-deep in the water. We said goodbye to Enzo, headed back to "Villa Sauna," and endured the ten-minute walk uphill to our room.

We showered, changed, and decided to have dinner near the shoreline because we'd spent twenty-two euros that day and just wanted to try it. We ate next to the club La Terrazza dei Leoni and sat outdoors, people watching. I ordered one of the specials, and Alejandra ordered a chicken dish. Our meals came out, and mine looked exactly like the one I'd had the previous night.

"Does my dish look like the same meal I had for dinner last night?" I asked Alejandra.

"Let me see. Yes, it does," Alejandra replied. "How does it taste?"

"Delicious. I just didn't think I ordered the same dish from last night?"

We finished our meals and walked around the shoreline, visited the shops, and headed back to "Villa Sauna." By the time we reached our room, I had sweated through my clothes. "I'm going to shower. I'm gross," I said.

"Are you going to give the night-time crowd a show?" Alejandra asked.

"The 2:30 p.m. show is totally different from the 9:30 p.m. show," I said.

She laughed. "I'll alert the media."

"You could shower with me to conserve water."

"You got some this morning," Alejandra stated.

"Is there some Italian law that I don't know about that says you can't have sex twice in one day?" I asked.

"Yes, paragraph four, sentence one of the Italian Bill of Rights clearly states, 'Men will only have sex once a day,'" Alejandra said with a straight face.

"That sucks. Glad I'm just visiting. I plan on starting a riot for my fellow Italian males, protesting this oppressive regime."

"Again, I'll alert the media," she said.

I showered. I didn't see any faces gawking at me this time, but how would I know? It was night, and only the shower was lit up.

When I got out of the shower, Alejandra was Facetiming her sister, Sue. I had the towel wrapped around me, though she could only see me from the neck up. "The kids are fine, nothing to worry about," Sue said.

Alejandra and Sue made small talk for fifteen minutes. Alejandra shut the computer down and came to bed. I put my hand on her ass, and she said, "We have to be up early, and you got some already."

"You're no fun," I said.

I went to sleep disappointed.

We woke at seven the next morning and were ready and out the door by seven thirty. We got our emotional-support beverages (coffee) and went to the local deli to buy sandwiches for Capri. The prosciutto was one euro—one fucking euro. It was five bucks back in the States! We ordered two prosciutto and mozzarella sandwiches for five euros. I felt like we should have been wearing ski masks; those sandwiches were a steal. We went across the road and down the steep stairway to the Capri booth to await our transport.

We met Emily at the dock with four other couples, and our boat arrived at port at 8:20 a.m. We checked in and boarded the boat for the fifty-minute ride to Capri. We docked at 9:10 and were informed by our hostess, Olivia, to "be at this dock at 1:00 p.m. sharp, otherwise, you will miss the rest of the tour and need to find another means of transportation to get back to Positano."

We adhered to her advice, exited the boat, and walked up a hill to a funicular railway car that was on a railroad track going up a forty-five-degree slope held by cables. It was part train, part cable car. We decided to take the railroad car for ten euros and waited for fifteen minutes to get on the car and up to the top of Capri. The view at the top of Capri was breathtaking, and we took a couple of panoramic photos of the island and a couple of us with the view in the background.

We exited the station and were immediately in the middle of a shopping square. On our right was a jewelry store, where the average watch cost 150,000 euros. In front of us was the five-star Hotel Caesar Augustus. We window-shopped, and I do mean window-shopped. Any buying of any items would have cost us our first born.

We walked around the island and visited a monastery to look around. We visited shops, ate our lunch on a park bench, and just took in the view. We headed back to the dock at 12:30.

At 1:00, the boat showed up, and everyone from our group boarded. Then we were off to the Blue Grotto. The captain brought the boat as far as it would go, and we were met by rowboat taxis. The two of us got in, and the taxi-boat driver brought us to a cashier, who was in a different boat. It was fifteen euros each to enter the Blue Grotto. I asked if they took Visa. They didn't, so we paid in cash and waited in line to enter a crack in a mountain about three feet wide and two feet high. Our taxi-boat driver, Claudio, told us to lay back so we wouldn't get decapitated. We obliged. He pushed us through, and we entered the Blue Grotto. It was amazing. The entire cave is blue, top to bottom, from the reflection of the water. It is almost psychedelic. We spent ten minutes and then exited the cave and went back to our boat. The thirty euros were well worth the experience.

We got everyone back on board and made a stop to take a dip into the Tyrrhenian Sea. I asked Alejandra, "Do you swim?"

She said, "Yes, why are you asking me such a dumb question?"

"Because in the seven years we've been together, I have never seen you go into the water above your kneecaps."

Alejandra laughed, and for the first time in our relationship, I saw her jump in the blue water of the Tyrrhenian Sea and start swimming. We spent ten minutes in the water before the captain hit the horn, signaling us to return so we could visit the green and white grottos. We came back on board and toweled off, enjoyed some hors d'oeuvres provided by the boat, and headed to the other grottos.

The green and white grottos weren't as spectacular as the Blue Grotto—probably the reason no one charged us to enter them, unlike the Blue Grotto. They were nice. "Not thrilling, but nice," to quote the great Mel Brooks.

On our way back to Positano, we made our second and final dip into the sea. Alejandra stayed on board this time, and I swam alone. In the water, I saw Alejandra holding a bottle of some sort of wine or champagne. I swam to the boat, and the captain and Olivia were serving champagne. This was fantastic. They turned music on, and everyone was having a good time.

We reached Positano, disembarked, and headed up to "Villa Sauna." We got undressed and showered separately, to my disappointment. Tonight's dinner was where we got dropped off by the bus. About two hundred feet from the bus stop was an outdoor restaurant overlooking the Tyrrhenian Sea. We ordered pasta dishes. The waitress came back and handed me the same dish I'd had yesterday and the day before.

"The name of this dish was different from last night, right?" I asked Alejandra.

"Yes, I believe so," Alejandra said.

"That's uncanny. I have ordered the same dish at three different restaurants, with three different names."

She laughed. "Only you."

"Yep, talk about lucky," I said.

After dinner, we walked around Positano before heading back to our room. It was 9 p.m., and we walked onto the balcony overlooking the beach of the Tyrrhenian Sea. It was pitch black outside; we couldn't see two feet in front of us. I grabbed Alejandra and kissed her hard on the lips. "Do you want to fuck outside?" I whispered in her ear.

"Yes," she said quietly.

And we proceeded to strip and start to go at it. Heavy groping and stroking—we started having sex. We were quiet, so the moans were soft. We didn't want to draw too much attention from our neighbors.

During our tryst outside, fireworks started coming from the beach, like you would see on the Fourth of July. Immediately, people started coming out of their villas to watch. We were mid-coitus when all the skies lit up and everyone got a different kind of show than they'd expected. We quickly stopped and retreated, crawling to our room laughing.

"That was embarrassing," Alejandra said, laughing.

"That was great!" I said.

"Besides the sex outside, why?" she asked.

"How awesome is it that fireworks were going off while we were doing the deed? It's like God was giving us the thumbs up, saying, 'Good job!'"

She laughed and saw that my soldier was still at full attention. She proceeded to service him in our bed. We fucked passionately while the fireworks exploded over our villa. God, I love Italy.

We spent our last day in Positano where we'd started—at the beach. We went back to Enzo's beach and enjoyed the sun and water. We left around 4 p.m. and headed back to our room in "Villa Sauna." We were online to check in for our flight from Rome to Newark Airport when Alejandra said, "We're not getting out tomorrow."

"What do you mean we're not getting out tomorrow?" I asked, concerned.

"Both flights are oversold by twenty," she replied.

"Can we connect from a different European city to

Newark?" I asked.

"I can check, but most flights to the States depart twice a day," Alejandra retorted.

"What if we stay in Italy an extra day?"

"Still no. Flights are oversold by twenty 'til Sunday," she said. "But let me work some magic and figure out where we are going."

Twenty minutes later, she said, "We are going to Germany."

12

Frankfurt, Germany

"GERMANY?" I ASKED.

"It's the only place in Europe we can get out of the following day. So, we will fly from Rome to Frankfurt, Germany, stay the night, and leave from Frankfurt to Newark the following day," Alejandra explained.

Alejandra bought discounted tickets from Lufthansa Airlines. The discounted tickets are half-price tickets for airline personnel so that if they have to fly on another carrier they don't have to pay the full price. We were leaving from Rome to Frankfurt at 11:30 a.m. the following day.

We packed and left "Villa Sauna," saying *ciao* to Giovanni. And yes, he was still wearing the same outfit from the first time we'd met him. Either he didn't have a washing machine, or he had seven sets of those exact same clothes in his closet.

We took a bus and two trains back to Rome and rented a room at a two-star hotel, so we could just sleep as we waited for our flight to Frankfurt. We checked in at 5 p.m. and put our things in our room to go have dinner. This time, I ordered a chicken dish and got an entirely different meal for the first time in four days.

We walked back to the hotel and stopped at a square where a street band was playing drums on plastic buckets. There was a crowd, and we decided to hang around and enjoy the Italian nightlife for one last time. We soaked up the atmosphere, music, and people for one final hurrah. We realized that our trip was almost over and that we soon had to go back to reality. We headed back to the room and proceeded to make love—yes, that's right: for the third time in our relationship, we made love, slow and steady. Like our animalistic sex, it was just fantastic.

We woke up early the following day and took a taxi to the airport. We went through security and had no problems since the flight to Frankfurt was wide open. We sat in the emergency exit row of the plane and answered the standard flight-attendant questions, like, "Are you willing to help in case of an emergency? If you are not willing to help or can't we will move you to another seat."

We answered yes and were now on the hook for being responsible for that exit.

The flight took off and the very sexy Lufthansa flight attendants came out to do the service. Did I say sexy? I didn't notice the short gray uniforms, red hats and scarfs, or black stockings. Total oversight by me.

Our flight attendant asked us if we would like anything to drink.

"I'll have a beer," I said.

She handed me a bottle of Spaten Munchen—a bottle! Unlike Global Airlines that gives you a can and a plastic cup. It was fantastic! Oh my God, the Germans know how to brew beer.

The flight was awesome, and we weren't even sitting in First Class. We were treated like royalty for the entire two-hour flight.

We landed and checked into the Frankfurt Airport Hilton Hotel, which looked like a space-age futuristic hotel with windows all over the place. We got to our room, and I did the perfunctory look inside. "It's clear," I said, and we went inside. I told Alejandra, "I'm going to the gym."

"Okay, have fun," she said as I changed into workout attire. I headed to the glass elevators and went down to the gym. I did some weights and cardio and went back to the room. In the ten days I'd been in Italy, I'd lost ten pounds because of the heat and humidity. I hadn't worked out one day.

"Where do you want to go eat for dinner?" Alejandra asked.

"No idea. Let me shower and get changed, and we'll go," I replied. "Did you shower, or do you want to save the environment?" I asked.

"I showered when you were working out, and you got some last night," she said.

"Just asking."

I showered and changed, and we headed out to eat. We looked around and found a bar/restaurant in the hotel. I ordered a hamburger and a beer, and Alejandra had the same. The waitress, Ella, came back with two huge beers in glass mugs. The mugs were about eight inches wide and twenty-four inches deep. You could've docked your jet ski in my beer. There was even an undertow.

"Holy shit, this thing is huge!" I said.

"That's what she said," Alejandra retorted.

I started cracking up. She got me with my own joke. "Look at this: it's got its own tide guide," I said.

Alejandra laughed, and we clinked glasses and drank our beers. Ella came back with our burgers, and they were huge too! "Did they just slay the cow outside and carve him out back?" I asked.

"This is a big burger," she agreed.

"I've heard of everything being bigger in Texas, but this trumps Texas."

Alejandra took offense because she's a Texas girl born and bred. "You may want to rephrase your answer, mister," she said.

"I'll rephrase, mea culpa: These are the biggest burgers and beers I have ever seen."

"Better."

We finished our food and beers, paid the bill, and walked back to our room. I was a little tipsy; drinking that one beer was like drinking three. We got back into the room, and I attacked Alejandra.

Alejandra said, "You got some yesterday."

"I did, but we are in Germany, a new country, and you know the rule: new country, we have to have sex in it," I said.

She laughed and said, "Make it fun, make it fast."

I followed her exact instructions and finished rather quickly. Not one of my better performances, but I was glad we did it—for the sanctity of the rule, of course.

Alejandra listed us for first class for our Frankfurt to Chicago flight, which left at 10 a.m. We would arrive at 2 p.m. Chicago time and connect to El Paso from Chicago. We should arrive in El Paso around 6 p.m. mountain time.

We arrived at Frankfurt Airport, sat down, and awaited our names to be called. The flight was wide open, and we got first class. Mr. and Mrs. Papagiorgio! Nothing like free drinks, unlimited movies, and a sundae to boot. Flying back to the States in style.

13

Heated Argument to Denver

ON DECEMBER 10, 2017, MY father-in-law, Raul, passed away after living to the ripe old age of ninety. As a family, we decided to have him cremated and hold his funeral in January of 2018 because we didn't want Christmas to end on a sad note with a funeral.

The first weekend of January, we would hold his funeral in Juarez, Mexico. I would miss a couple of days of work, but they would be excused, and Alejandra's trips would automatically be picked up by Global Airlines. Global Airlines also made sure that we didn't have to fly standby when we travelled to and from El Paso, making us positive space passengers, meaning we were automatically on the plane even before the paying passengers.

We were going to leave on Thursday, January 4, but the weather was not cooperating.

"Love, we may want to change our flight plans," I yelled from the kitchen as I watched the weather report on the television.

"Why?" she called back from our room.

"The weathermen are saying there is a bomb cyclone coming through here on Thursday, saying it's going to drop a foot of snow and be negative ten out."

She ran from the bedroom to the TV and caught the last part of the weather report. She quickly jumped on the phone with her supervisor. "Simon, is there any way we can get on the Wednesday flight to El Paso because of the weather? Otherwise, I'm missing my father's funeral."

"No problem. I'll book you on the 10 a.m. flight to Denver," Simon replied.

"Thank you, Simon," Alejandra said gratefully. She turned to me and said, "We're leaving tomorrow. Take care of your lesson plans for work and pack for yourself. I have to finish packing for the kids." Alejandra said to me.

"Okay, I'll get it done."

Alejandra and the kids would pick me up at school thanks to a colleague's picking me up and driving me to work, giving Alejandra time to pack and make sure we had everything. At 3 p.m., I exited the sea of students, crossed the railroad tracks by my school, and hopped in the car to go to Newark Airport. We arrived at the airport, checked our luggage all the way to El Paso curbside, went through security, and received our tickets at the gate. It was a full flight, but we had seats, although not together. I was sitting behind my youngest daughter, Allie (named after my wife Alejandra) and Alejandra, while Jack and Sophia were sitting together three rows up. Two-year-old Allie was having a major meltdown. Yes, we are that family that everyone wants to sit next to.

Luckily, my wife and I came prepared. We had tons of Global Airlines drink tickets and handed them out to everyone in a three-row radius of us. When the flight attendant came around for drink orders, we heard, "I'll have a beer," "I'll have a red wine," and watched as they gladly handed in their free drink tickets to the flight attendant.

The woman next to me in the aisle seat, a white-haired lady in her late sixties, said she didn't want one.

"Okay, no worries."

Mid-way through the flight, Alejandra had to use the bathroom and told me to take over. Allie was having a rough flight. She was exhausted, couldn't find her place, was screaming, and when her mother went to the bathroom by herself, she threw the biggest temper tantrum imaginable. I was doing everything I could do to calm her down. A gentleman in his late sixties came up to me and said, "Shut her up!"

I said, "Excuse me?"

"You heard me: shut her up! She's giving me a headache from all of her screaming," he shouted.

Out came all the cameras. Youtube, Twitter, Snapchat, here I come. If I hit this guy, I would go to jail, and Alejandra would lose her job with Global Airlines. I would also lose my job as a teacher, because if I got arrested for assault, no matter how good an excuse I had, they'd say I should know better. This all ran through my head within a few seconds.

I said sternly, "Go back to your seat, sir."

"Make me," he said.

In a voice calm but stern, I said to him, "If I get up from my seat, you're going to have a bigger problem than being arrested when the flight lands. You're going to need serious medical attention when I'm done with you. So, I'll ask you again to go back to your seat."

"Are you threatening me?" he asked.

"No, I'm promising you. That is what is going to happen."

The total time of this "discussion" was three minutes. He returned to his seat, and Alejandra came back from the bathroom and said, "You look like you want to kill someone. What happened?"

My daughter Sophia, "the Informer," told Mom everything that happened. Immediately, Alejandra lost it. "Point him out to me, I'll say something to him!" Her Latina temper was on overdrive.

"Alejandra, I handled it. There is no need to keep it going. He won't be coming back here."

"How do you know that? Well, what did you say to him?"

I explained what transpired. "I still want to give him a piece of my mind," she said.

"Don't. He's not worth it. But if he does come back, I promise you won't get a shot at him, because I'm going to be all over him," I said.

The woman next to me on the aisle got up and walked over to the man who yelled at Allie. The older gentleman did not look back.

Allie fell asleep with an hour left in the flight. We landed, and the bell to let everyone know it was okay to walk around the cabin sounded. The woman in the aisle seat sprinted to the man who yelled at Allie. Apparently, she was his wife, sitting next to me the entire flight. She got scared because I'd said, "If that son of a bitch comes near anyone from my family, I'm going to knock his ass out."

The man did not look back, collected his luggage from the overhead compartment, and walked off the plane with his wife. People sitting across from me, behind me, and in front of me were slapping me on the back, saying, "Man, you handled that great. I don't think I could have done what you just did. You are one cool customer."

"Thanks, I would have hit him, but he's not worth me or my wife getting arrested by Federal Air Marshals," I replied.

Now the fun part: did the asshole change the story and say I'd harassed him? Were there air marshals or the Denver police department outside the gate?

We were the last ones off the plane because there were five of us, and I was carrying Allie, who was still asleep. We exited the plane. No air marshals. We waited for our black stroller at the bottom of the jetway. It came up, we put Allie in it, and we walked up the jetway to go to our next gate. We were at the top of the jetway—no police, no elderly couple, nothing. In fact, we didn't see that elderly couple ever again.

14

Roswell, New Mexico

IN SUMMER OF 2017, WE headed to El Paso to spend time with my in-laws. In August, I finished summer school, which was an English jumpstart program for high school seniors becoming college freshmen at the local community college where I teach as an adjunct professor. The last two weeks of August were reserved for visiting the family in Texas.

As usual, there were problems getting to El Paso because as I stated earlier, there are no direct flights from Newark there. We usually flew through Denver, Houston, or Chicago. Unfortunately, when all of those options were full, we went to our fourth and fifth option, Austin or Dallas, with a ten- to twelve-hour drive or another flight, using ID-90s on another airline.

It's kind of like being a quarterback. Your prime receiver is Houston. He's your best option, but he's usually double covered. Your second receiver is Denver, a sure-handed receiver, not as good as Houston, but reliable. Your third receiver is Chicago.

He's good on third down, but he drops the ball too many times to become a prime receiver. Austin is your tight end. He's reliable, but he's not going to give you much after the catch. If you want ten yards, he'll get you ten yards. If you want twelve yards, he'll still get you ten yards. Finally, there is Dallas. He's your check-down running back. You throw the ball to him only if everyone else is covered, and you expect only five yards at the most.

Today, everybody was covered. There were no flights to get to our first destination to El Paso. We chose Dallas because it was the only open flight to Texas. I was expecting to buy discounted tickets to El Paso on Patriotic Airlines or to take a ten-hour drive through Texas with three kids under the age of seven in the backseat. Note to the reader: I have driven this trip and would rather take a flight to the middle of nowhere.

We landed in Dallas, and Alejandra gave her "airline sister," Ciara, a family friend whom I've known since birth, a call to ask about connections to El Paso. Since Ciara was a retired flight attendant for Patriotic Airlines, she could still fly standby on her airline and had access to the system to let us know about flights.

"It's oversold by seven," Ciara said. "Buying discounted tickets would make you guys eight through thirteen."

"Damn it," Alejandra said.

"Wait a minute. You could fly to Roswell, New Mexico. How far out is that from El Paso?" Ciara asked.

"About three and a half hours," Alejandra said. "When does it leave Dallas, and how many open seats does it have?"

"It leaves at 9:30 p.m., puts you into Roswell at 11:00 p.m. It's wide open."

"Okay. Let me call Sue to see if she can pick us up from there. Thanks for your help," Alejandra said.

"No problem, anytime."

Alejandra phoned Sue and told her the plan.

"Alex will come and get you," Sue said. "Just text us before you leave so he can leave here. This way he's not waiting around if you get delayed. There is nothing around there, he says."

Alex went to a military academy in Roswell to play baseball before he blew out his shoulder.

"Okay, will do," Alejandra said.

Alejandra bought the discounted tickets online, and we waited for two hours by the gate in Dallas Airport. The gate to Roswell was out of the way, where all the "Barbie jets" flew into. A "Barbie jet" is a small fifty-seater plane. We were a half hour away from departing and seated at the gate. My seven-year-old son, Jack, was bored, so he dug in his carry-on bag, which is a black Darth Vader roller board, and put on his cape with the "J" and a lightning bolt on the back, turning himself into SuperJack and running up and down the terminal. Sophia saw him, dug in her pink Barbie roller board, and put on her pink lightning bolt Cape with an "S" on it, and became SuperSophia. Who knew there was this much crime in the airport? Allie was two and just watched them. Other customers were watching and laughing. We let them run, knowing it would tire them out and make the ride to Roswell easier.

The Patriotic Airlines gate agent arrived an hour before the flight departed, and Alejandra worked her magic to start up a friendship with Katherine. Katherine and Alejandra became fast friends, and Katherine gave us our tickets to Roswell. What's the old saying? Be careful what you wish for? We were headed to Roswell, New Mexico. Nowhere, I believe I said, I would rather fly to than drive across Texas. Keep your mouth shut from now on, C. J.

We got our tickets from Katherine and sat together, three across on one side and two across the aisle. Alejandra sent a text to Sue, saying, "We're on the plane, scheduled to arrive on time. Tell Alex to come and get us."

"Okay, see you soon, sister," Sue replied.

The flight to Roswell was a smooth one, and everyone including Allie slept for the hour-and-thirty-five-minute flight. We landed at 11:00 p.m. mountain time and, as always, were the last ones to leave the plane because we usually have more stuff and people to deplane with. We got our black stroller at the bottom of the jetway, put Allie in it, and were on our way to the top of the jetway and into Roswell Airport. We emerged from the jetway, and holy shit was this airport small—and when I say small, I mean there was one rent-a-car dealership, and it was closed. There wasn't a restaurant in the airport—just vending machines. And I thought El Paso International Airport was tiny! An elderly gentleman at the top of the jetway said, "The airport will be closing in five minutes."

"Closing?"

"Yes, sir, till six tomorrow morning."

"So, where do we go?" I asked.

"There are benches and an overhang outside. You can sit there 'til you get picked up," he said.

"Can we go to the bathroom first, before you kick us out?" I asked politely.

"Sure."

Five minutes later, we were literally kicked out of Roswell Airport by the elderly gentleman as he wrapped chains around the handles of the glass doors and locked them. We were joined by two other families outside. Luckily, it was eighty degrees, so we didn't have to brave the elements.

The kids were now fully awake and running around in front of Alejandra and me. Alejandra texted Alex, who was about an hour and a half away from the airport. The kids were occupied, and I slept about an hour.

Literally ninety minutes later, Alex rolled up in his blue Honda Pilot, and the kids ran to give him hugs and kisses. We put our luggage in the back and climbed in. We were making small talk when he said, "C. J., I have been driving for a while. Can you take over in an hour?"

"I don't know where we are going," I said.

"I'll get us to I-10 East. Once I do that, you can take over. It's a straight shot to Santa Teresa from there," he said.

"How long of a drive from once we get on I-10 to your house?" I asked.

"Three hours."

"Three hours. I'm on fumes right now. I've only slept an hour, and it's 2:30 in the morning my time, but I'll try."

"Thanks," he replied.

An hour passed, and Alex got us to I-10 East. I'd tried getting some sleep but couldn't. We pulled the car over in a short mall parking lot and changed places. Alex was a big guy—over six feet and 230 pounds. I had to adjust the seat and face a steering wheel with a Dallas Cowboys cover. "Really, dude?" I pointed to the steering wheel.

He laughed. "I had to."

"I'll have to wipe my hands with a disinfectant wipe after this," I said. I was a die-hard New York Giants fan, and if there was anything I couldn't stand, it was the Dallas Cowboys. Well played, Alex, well played.

I drove on I-10 East, which as I have stated before is the "Hypnosis Highway." It's just straight. Unfortunately, Alejandra was sitting in the back with the kids, and my brother-in-law was riding shotgun. There was no chance for a blow job this time.

Two hours in, I started getting tired and nodding off. I opened the window so I could wake up. I smacked myself hard in the face, twice, so the pain would keep me awake.

"C. J., are you okay?" Alejandra asked.

"I'm just trying to keep myself awake. I'm tired."

"I'll keep you awake," she said, and started making small talk with Alex and me.

It was a struggle to keep my eyes open, and I could barely see straight, but we finally made it to Alex's house safely. We dropped him off because he had to work in the morning, and Sue came out to greet us. We said hello and goodbye because we were staying at my mother-in-law's house. It was 3 a.m. mountain time, 5 a.m. eastern time. Alejandra climbed into the driver's seat and drove the last thirty minutes to El Paso to her mother's house.

15

Los Angeles

"DO YOU WANT TO VISIT my brother, Rudy, in LA for the weekend for Spring Break and then head to El Paso? He wants to meet you," Alejandra asked.

"Sure, why not," I replied.

It was April 2007, and Alejandra and I were getting very serious with our relationship. I was meeting her half-brother, Rudy, and his wife, Janet, and Alejandra's father again. Obviously, this would be interesting.

"Where are we staying? Hotel?" I asked.

"No, Rudy wants us to stay with him," Alejandra replied.

"I don't want to intrude. We can get a room in LA."

"He insists."

"Okay."

We left on Saturday, March 31, at 7 a.m. out of Newark Airport on Global Airlines and took the six-hour flight to Los Angeles. The flight was wide open, and we sat in coach and slept most of the way.

We arrived in LAX at 10:20 a.m., and Rudy picked us up at the airport in his BMW. Inside the car with Rudy was Alejandra and Rudy's dad, Raul, riding shotgun. Alejandra and I sat in the backseat.

Rudy lived in Anaheim, literally two blocks away from Angel Stadium of Anaheim. We passed it on the way to his house. "Rudy, how many games do you get to a year?" I asked.

"About twenty to thirty," he said. "If I have nothing to do, I'll buy a bleacher seat and walk to and from the game."

"That's awesome," I said. "I would do the same if I lived this close to Yankee Stadium."

"I see all the good teams, the Yankees, the Red Sox, everyone," he said. "I took Dad to the last Yankees game here. He's a big baseball fan." (He then translated to Raul, who didn't speak a word of English.)

Raul nodded his head in agreement.

We arrived at Rudy's house in Anaheim, and it was beautiful. He showed us to our room, which looked like the jungle. The walls were all green, and the bed was a queen with a four-post canopy and green sheets and bedspread. I wondered if, if we made a lot of noise while we were fucking, they would think it was jungle animals.

We put our luggage down, and Alejandra asked, "Where's Janet?"

"She's working. You'll see her tonight for dinner," Rudy said.

We got back in the BMW and headed to brunch at a nice place overlooking the water. We had a nice meal. I had three twelve-ounce Arnold Palmers (half iced tea, half lemonade). I didn't use the restroom, because we were ten minutes away from Rudy's house. What could possibly happen during a ten-minute time span?

On our way to Rudy's house, Rudy got a phone call from Janet, which he took on speaker.

"Do you want to take Alejandra and C. J. to a magical place where dreams happen and from there meet me for dinner?" Janet asked.

Before I got two words out of my mouth, Rudy responded, "Sure, we'll see you at six."

He turned the car onto the freeway, heading to a magical place where dreams happen. With every pothole Rudy hit, my bladder was about to burst over my white khaki pants. I whispered to Alejandra, "I have to pee . . . bad."

"Can you hold it?" she asked.

"Not much longer."

"Rudy, how far out are we?" Alejandra asked.

"About ten minutes. Why?"

"C. J. has to pee."

I immediately turned red. I tried to think about anything dry, but every bump, stop, dip, and dive made my bladder beg for relief.

We were about to go into the magical place where dreams come true, and Rudy slowed down. On my right was an open parking garage, and all I had to do was get out of the car, hop over the concrete divider, and piss anywhere I could find a spot.

Rudy slowed the car down. This was my chance. The car stopped, and I opened the backdoor, got out, and signaled to Alejandra that I'd text her inside by using my left hand and thumb. I hopped the divider, and there were cameras everywhere. I looked for a corner, but there were none to be found. I decided to pee between two parked cars. I pulled my dick out and a family of six came walking directly toward me. I hadn't pissed yet, but I had to abort my plan. I went three cars down, looked left and right, unleashed Mr. Happy. Finally, relief. If sex is the best feeling in the world, taking a wicked leak is a close second. I pissed for literally four minutes. It was awesome. I finished and felt like a new man. Alejandra texted me, "When you're done, we're at the gate of the park."

I jogged to the park entrance and found Rudy, Raul, and Alejandra laughing at me. I blushed.

"If you had to go that bad, I would have pulled over," Rudy said.

"Sorry about that," I said apologetically.

"Don't worry about it."

We went into the park and had a good time. Three hours later, we left the park, and Rudy asked me, "Do you need to go to the bathroom? It's a thirty-minute drive to the restaurant."

"I'm good," I said.

"You're sure?" he asked sarcastically.

"I'm good," I reiterated. Everyone is a fucking comedian.

Thirty minutes later, we arrived at the Outlets of Orange, an outdoor mall, and dined at a seafood restaurant called the Market Broiler. I met Janet, Rudy's wife. She was beautiful inside and out and very welcoming. We had a great meal and made small talk around the table. The peeing incident from earlier in the day came up, and everyone laughed, including me, though again I blushed.

We left the restaurant, and, yes, I did go to the bathroom before we got into Janet's car. Rudy took his dad, Raul, back to his hotel. We entered the house, and Alejandra and I said goodnight to Janet because it was now 11 p.m. east coast time. In the "Jungle Room," we got out of our clothes and finally washed the airplane gunk off. We showered separately, to my disappointment, then got to bed. Yes, I wanted to have sex with Alejandra, but we were both tired and fell asleep quickly.

The next morning was much different: Alejandra woke me up properly with a blow job. If I may ask the obvious, is there a better way to wake up a man? I snapped out of my slumber, and we went at it, hard, with lots of moaning and groaning. Hey, we were in the "Jungle Room."

We finished up and made ourselves presentable to have breakfast with Rudy and Janet.

That day, Rudy and Janet took us all over Anaheim to sightsee, and we had a fantastic time. That night, we checked flights to El Paso, and since nothing was going out of LAX for standby, we tried John Wayne Airport in Santa Ana, which was closer to Rudy's house than LAX. Global Airlines flew out of John Wayne Airport, so we could catch a ride to El Paso from there, with the flight open at ten. We'd have no problem getting on the flight, we thought.

We woke up the next morning and checked the flights, it was at two. Rudy took us to the airport, and we went through security with no problem and checked our luggage at the curb. We headed to the gate, and Alejandra asked the gate agent, "How do the flights look to El Paso?"

"Full, we're at negative five."

"Negative five! It was positive two, two hours ago," Alejandra said.

"Well, they filled up," Stephanie said.

Alejandra came over to me and said, "It's now negative five. We're not getting on this flight. Get on the computer."

"Negative five? What, are they giving away free blow jobs in El Paso today?" I exclaimed.

"Apparently," she said.

I fired up the computer, and Alejandra logged onto Global Airlines. All the flights to El Paso were oversold, but not by much.

Negative two or three at the most. The next flight was 10:15 a.m., and since we didn't make the 8 a.m. flight, we were now three and four on the standby list.

I got us some coffees after we moved to the next gate for El Paso. I came back and handed Alejandra her coffee, and we waited until they started boarding. It was going to be close, but we might actually make it. The gate agent started calling names. "Thomas?"

"Here." A man and woman appeared in front of the gate agent, who gave them their tickets.

Alejandra asked the gate agent, "Any more standbys?"

"No, it's now full. You'll roll over for the next flight at one."

The door closed, the plane pushed back, and we moved over to the next El Paso gate to wait. We again fired up the computer. We were three on the list, and the flight was still negative four.

We got lunch and waited until the gate agent started boarding. A couple with three kids under the age of five were lugging their bags to a gate. The father of the family had two car seats strapped together with a cord and thrown over his back to carry. He and his wife looked exhausted. Alejandra saw the family, looked at me, and said, "That will be us in five years."

"Great. Can't wait," I said.

She laughed. The boarding process started, and this time no standbys got on. We were again rolled over to the next flight at 3:30. We had been in John Wayne Airport since 6:30 a.m. We were number eight on the standby list.

"Is there any other way we can get to El Paso?" I asked.

"I'll check."

She went to routing and looked at all the airports near LA: Tucson, Phoenix, Denver. Everything was oversold. We were not getting out.

"What if we went north?" I asked.

"North?"

"San Francisco."

"I'll try." She input the route. It was open to San Francisco and from San Francisco to El Paso.

"The San Francisco flight is wide open and leaves at 4 p.m., and the El Paso flight is open by five and leaves at seven" Alejandra explained.

"List us," I said.

She did, and we moved to the San Francisco gate. At the gate, Alejandra spoke with the gate agent and got the tickets to San Francisco. She smiled and handed me my ticket.

"Finally," I said.

"I know. The joys of non-revving."

"I'm just glad we are getting on."

We took the hour-and-thirty-five-minute flight to San Francisco. We landed at 5:45 p.m. and hustled to make our El Paso connection. We got to the gate as they were boarding first class passengers.

Out of breath, Alejandra asked the gate agents, "Have you cleared standbys yet?"

"Not yet," he said.

With ten minutes left for boarding, he called, "Nicholas, Sanchez?"

"Right here," we said.

"Here you go." He handed us our tickets, and we ran down the jetway to our seats on the Barbie jet to El Paso.

We sat next to each other and stowed our carry-ons.

"We spent twelve hours in the airport and in the air," I said.

"I'm glad we are heading home," she said. Although we live in New Jersey, Alejandra still considers El Paso home.

"The joys of non-revving," I said.

16

Italy with the Family

IN APRIL OF 2019, JACK told Alejandra and me that he wanted to go to Italy for his tenth birthday. Now, normally I would think to myself, "And I want to be in a hot threesome with your mother and any one of her hot female friends, but it's just not in the cards." But since I lived with a flight attendant, we could make this happen. The only fly in the ointment was our four-year-old, Allie. Allie had been flying with us since she was conceived, but our problem was that Europe really isn't kid-friendly. It's stairs, walking, public transportation, time change, weather— not really the ideal place for a toddler. Side note: we had always wanted to take the kids to Europe but figured we would do it when they were teenagers.

We told Jack, "We can take you and Sophia with us, but maybe Grandma and Aunt Suzanne could watch Allie for ten days."

Jack freaked out. "Either we all go, or none of us go. She is my sister, and I will not leave without her."

"Jack, Allie isn't the easiest child in our family. Are you going to carry her and comfort her when she has a meltdown?" Alejandra asked Jack. Side note: the worst day of Allie's life will be the day she does not cry about something.

"I will take care of her, and we either all go, or none go," Jack said through tears.

Alejandra said, "We'll think about it," to calm Jack down.

I followed Alejandra into our bedroom and said, "If you're serious about taking them to Italy, then Jack has a point."

"Really? You know Allie is going to be difficult on that trip. You have been to Rome before. All the walking—Allie can't do that."

"I understand that, but what have we said to Jack over and over again? We're a family, and we stick together. We've instilled this into him since he was two," I explained. "I agree with him: we need to bring Allie."

"Fine, but you are going to handle all the meltdowns and temper tantrums," Alejandra said.

"Okay, no worries."

Alejandra went into planning mode and started looking at flights, which were wide open because it was April and we weren't leaving until late August. She also researched Airbnbs in Bologna, Rome, and Florence. She used maps to figure how long it would take us to go here on this day and there on another day and the radius of this city versus that city. Highly scientific stuff.

We settled on an Airbnb in Bologna, thinking it was close to Florence and Rome, where we would spend a couple of days. Then we'd go to Venice for two days, and then head to Rome for the rest of our vacation. I use the word *thinking* because we were dead wrong on being close to Rome.

Alejandra booked the Airbnbs in both Bologna and Rome,

and we planned to fly standby to Rome. We were supposed to leave on Thursday, August 15, at 6 p.m., but as with all flights in which you non-rev on, things change at a moment's notice. Two weeks out, flights were wide open. One week out, flights were filling up. Two days before, Alejandra said, "Flights are full. I'm booking us to Venice, and we can take a train to Bologna from there."

"You're the boss," I replied, and it was true. Being married to a flight attendant, I understood any travel itinerary should be set by her. She was the expert.

Alejandra listed us for Venice. The night before, we picked up a travel stroller from Alejandra's friend Laura for Allie. It was old but in working condition, and we packed it in our white Nissan Pathfinder.

We arrived at the airport parking lot in plenty of time, parked our car, got on the employee bus, went through security with no problem, and ordered dinner for our kids while we waited to see if we made the flight.

The flights had filled up since that morning, and there was no guarantee that we were getting on this flight as the five of us. "We may have to break up and meet you there," Alejandra said.

"We all go, or we all stay," I said. "I'm not splitting the family up."

"Hopefully we all get on."

Ten minutes left till boarding, we heard over the loudspeaker, "Nicholas, party of five."

Alejandra went up with our passports and pointed to us as she talked and worked her magic with the gate agent. She came back and said, "Okay, we're split up on the plane, but you're right in front of us in coach. You, Jack, and Sophia are together, while Allie and I are behind you."

We got on the plane, situated ourselves in our seats, and then took a family selfie before we departed to Venice, Italy.

The flight went well, and I was able to sleep a little—about two hours, tops. Jack, Sophia, and even Allie slept throughout the flight as well. We arrived in Venice, Italy, without much fanfare, went through immigration, and looked for the train to take an hour-and-a-half ride to Bologna. We got to the train station from the airport and grabbed a quick bite to eat.

We were the quintessential American family with six bags of luggage, a stroller, and four carry-ons walking through the train station. By the look of us, any person could say, "Look at the Americans!"

When we arrived in Bologna, it was ninety degrees and sunny, but we had one small problem: contacting the host of our Airbnb. Since we didn't have international service on our American phones, we needed Wi-Fi. We took a three-block walk and found our apartment, which was right next to a bar that was on vacation for the next three weeks.

We all walked to the busiest street at the end of the block, made a left, and went all the way to the end to a cafe. Alejandra, who is fluent in Italian, asked the manager, "*Hai* Wi-Fi?"

"*Si, signora,*" the mid-forties gentleman replied.

She ordered five waters and asked for the Wi-Fi passcode, then dialed our host's number.

"*Si, si. Ciao,*" Alejandra said. "He'll be at the apartment in twenty minutes."

We sat, finished our waters, and left with ten minutes to go due to our massive amounts of luggage. It was difficult to leave the air-conditioned cafe, but we headed out into the heat and back to the entrance of our apartment, waiting on an empty street. Five minutes later, our host arrived and let us into the apartment building.

We took a three-person max elevator to the fifth floor. Since we had a ton of luggage, Alejandra, Allie, and our host, Francesco, went up while Sophia, Jack, and I waited with the luggage. The elevator arrived in the lobby, and I sent Jack and Sophia along with one piece of luggage. I told Jack, "When you get out of the elevator, send it back down with you in it, and we'll unload the luggage this way."

"Got it, Dad," Jack replied.

Up they went. I heard the elevator stop five floors above, stop, and then return back downstairs with Jack. We did this three more times until all the luggage was in the apartment. The apartment was extremely hot and stuffy, and Alejandra opened the windows so we could get some air. It was a beautiful, spacious six-room apartment with a living room, eat-in kitchen, full bathroom, laundry room, and two bedrooms.

Francesco told us that only the master bedroom had air-conditioning. There were fans in the kid's bedroom and a cot in the main bedroom, which Jack claimed upon arrival. So much for having sex with Alejandra this vacation.

Francesco gave us the keys and told us where the nearest supermarket was before he departed. We undressed, showered, put our clothes in the washer, cranked the air-conditioning to its highest setting, and napped for five hours to help adjust to the time change.

We woke up and hung the wet laundry all over the place because there wasn't a dryer, for why would you need one in Casa De Sole (House of Sun)? I visited the supermarket and bought food, water, and snacks. After I'd returned and put away all the groceries, we strolled to Saint Peter Cathedral to catch some of the sights of Bologna.

We got to the Cathedral and walked around. In the back, we

could walk up the bell tower for five euros each. We decided to do it, parked our stroller, and climbed the 230-foot bell tower. What they don't tell you about the Bell Tower is that it's a one-way path about two-feet wide on a forty-five-degree incline with no steps or handrail! That's right. Apparently, someone invented the step and handrail in the fourteenth century. Since our entire family was wearing flip-flops with little to no traction, it was an interesting climb. They also forget to mention that people are coming down from the top of the bell tower and that we would literally have to turn our bodies so that everyone could get by or duck into a twelve-inch alcove where they would put candles at night. Apparently, the person descending has the right-of-way because it's more treacherous on the way down, which we would find out.

We reached the apex of the bell tower, saw the four bells in the tower, and listened to the tour guide's fifteen-minute speech (the tour guide stayed at the top and did not climb or descend until he was relieved by another tour guide). We looked as if we had just run a marathon, and we were sweating profusely. I'd carried everyone's plastic bottles in my backpack, and we drank and listened as we sat under one of the bells.

After listening to the speech and taking pictures of the family and some breathtaking views of Bologna, we had to descend the steep incline to return to the ground floor. I told Alejandra, "I'll go first and have Allie behind me. Have Sophia go next, then Jack, and you bring up the rear. Most importantly, be careful and go slowly."

To descend the 230 feet of a constant forty-five-degree angle, the Italians who constructed this bell tower put little speed bumps about an inch to two inches high every foot so you can stop. I put my left foot on the speed bump and turned it inward so I could balance myself with my hands out touching the walls.

Once I had my balance, I took Allie's hand and brought her next to me. It took us about a half hour to get to the bottom. To say no one fell would be correct; to say I almost fell five times would be an understatement. When we finally reached the ground, I felt like kissing it.

After the bell tower, we visited the Fountain of Neptune and listened to street musicians who played drums on plastic bins. There were about 200 people watching the very talented Italian gentlemen rock out for whatever spare change the crowd would give them. A detriment to this is that all the pickpockets make their way through like sharks to blood in the water. I noticed a bearded man following me. Every time I stopped, he stopped and looked in a different direction. What this Italian pickpocket didn't know was that I'm from New Jersey and I'd spotted him when we were watching the band play. He was standing diagonally to my right, behind me. Eventually, I stared at him and gave him a look that said, "I know what you are trying to do, and you are doing a horrible job of it. Go away before I hurt you." Apparently, this look is universal in any language, and he decided to leave.

The family and I headed back to our apartment after having dinner and gelato. We showered because it was over ninety degrees outside and probably 105 in our apartment. When we finished showering, we did another load of laundry. The good news about having a hot, stuffy apartment was that our clothes from the plane ride were completely dry. The bad news was that when we started the laundry, boom, the power went out. Clearly, you cannot run the laundry and the air-conditioning at the same time. Since, we now had no Wi-Fi, we couldn't contact Francesco. Alejandra said, "You are going to have to find a hotspot and contact Francesco to tell him what happened."

"Where am I going to do that?" I asked.

"I don't know. Find a place."

I was in white athletic shorts. I put on a shirt, took Alejandra's phone, and looked for a hotspot. The elevator was working, so there was power in the building. My first choice was the hotel across the street. Unfortunately, it was closed due to vacation and wouldn't open up until we left Bologna and headed for Rome.

I walked down our barren street and headed to the cafe where we'd had water and first made contact with Francesco. Strike two. It was closed and wouldn't reopen till tomorrow morning. I walked the main road and toward the Fountain of Neptune, where we'd just come from. After two blocks, I spotted a hotel on my right. I stepped into the lobby and looked down at Alejandra's phone. I had Wi-Fi. I immediately opened What's App and told Francesco what had happened. Ten minutes later, Francesco replied that he'd come first thing tomorrow morning. I said thank you, and walked out of the lobby of "Hotel Free Wi-Fi."

I arrived back at the apartment, and the kids and Alejandra hugged me as if I'd come back from war. I hugged them and said, "What's the matter?"

"We were worried about you. You were gone for forty-five minutes," Alejandra said.

"It took me a while to find free Wi-Fi," I said. "He's coming first thing tomorrow. We can't use the air-conditioning and the washer at the same time."

"Good to know," Alejandra said.

17

Broken Stroller in Venice, Italy

I KNOW WHAT YOU'RE THINKING: "Man, you must be made of money! Bologna, Florence, Venice, and Rome! How did you afford that?" When we make an itinerary, it is very dollar-specific and budgeted to the penny. We are by no means millionaires or upper class, but we are expert budgeters. Our Airbnbs are not going to be on *Lifestyles of the Rich and Famous* anytime soon. They are literally the bare necessities.

Like going to Venice for a day—Alejandra did this one on a whim. She's very spontaneous. It starts just like this: "Babe, I don't know what I was thinking; why we didn't stay in Venice when we flew in from Newark? But I researched an Airbnb, and it's eighty euros for the night and clean."

"Sure, do it. How much will it put us back in our budget?"

"Well, it's either this or Pisa."

"Venice."

We took a train back to Venice and a taxi to our Airbnb. It was still technically part of the city of Venice but away from the water. From where our Airbnb was located in Venice, we needed to take a bus to the water section that you see in so many movies and then walk that section of the city or take a boat.

But I digress. We arrived at our Airbnb, and it was exactly as Alejandra explained: clean, two bedrooms, and no kitchen. Wait, no kitchen? What kind of fucking apartment doesn't have a fucking kitchen? We were in the land of incredible architecture and spectacular food. Who was the genius architect who said, "You know what? Let's not build a kitchen. People don't eat." Brilliant! They should put him in the architecture Hall of Fame for that! At least there was a bathroom and a shower.

We met our host, Guiseppe, who gave us the key. We put our luggage down and walked to a cafe to buy bus tickets to and from the water part of Venice.

We bought our tickets and boarded everyone and the borrowed stroller, which Allie sat in until she spotted her brother and sister sitting in grown up seats and wanted to sit with them. We arrived at the stop and walked over the very lengthy footbridge. Allie had to get up and let me carry the strolled up and down the steps of the bridge. I should also say I was carrying a twenty-pound backpack and it was ninety degrees with 100 percent humidity. To say I was sweating like a pig would be an understatement.

What I did not know about Venice is that there are hundreds of *pontes* (bridges), so pushing Allie in a stroller was an exercise in futility. Every thirty-eight feet, I had to get her out of the stroller, hold her hand, and carry the stroller up and over the *ponte*; then I had to put her back in the stroller—all while dodging oncoming crowds. For the many times I accidentally knocked people with the stroller, I was not a popular person in Venice. (If you're one of the victims, let me sincerely apologize to you now.)

On one of the smaller *pontes*, I tripped, and the stroller hit one of the higher steps and smashed into my chest, leaving a nice mark and jamming my thumb in the impact. When I reached the bottom of the *ponte*, I put Allie back into the stroller, which started collapsing on her. I took her out and looked it over to discover that the screw by the front left wheel was bent. "Fuck me," I thought.

"The stroller is broken," I told Alejandra.

"How'd that happen?" she asked.

I told her, and although she wasn't happy with me, she really couldn't fault me either.

It was hot, humid, and now I had to carry Allie everywhere when she was tired. Alejandra pushed the broken stroller.

We visited St. Mark's Cathedral, which was magnificent, and then St. Mark's Square, where the kids played "Let's chase the pigeons!" It's an exciting game of three children chasing any pigeon they see in a ten-foot radius.

After watching the kids run around for fifteen minutes, we decided to eat dinner at a local restaurant with a view of the Adriatic Sea and the music drifting from St. Mark's Square.

We then walked back to the bus station to get to our Airbnb and crowded onto the bus. Allie and I were sitting next to each other, and Alejandra was sitting next to Sophia. Jack was sitting next to two stunning Italian women in their mid-twenties wearing very short-cut dresses. They had long black hair, tanned skin, and slim hourglass figures. Not that I saw them—I was just watching Jack to make sure he was okay.

Alejandra, who knew I had a wandering eye, noticed and said;

"What are you looking at?"

"Jack," I said in a normal what-kind-of-question-is-that tone.

"You are staring at those two Italian women over there, next to Jack," Alejandra said.

"There are two women by him?" I said, shocked.

"Yes, there are, and you know damn well what you are doing, mister," she replied.

"You mean the two tan-skinned, long black-haired, brown-eyed, Italian women in their mid-twenties wearing short dresses?"

"Yes, those," Alejandra said agitatedly.

"I didn't see them, but thank you for pointing them out to me." She laughed. "You're incorrigible."

"It's why you married me," I retorted. "I make you laugh."

"Yes, but for other reasons too," she said, giving me a seductive look.

"I'll apologize tonight," I said.

"You better."

We got home, showered, and put the kids to bed. We finally got in bed, and Alejandra said, "Make it fun, make it fast."

"You make it so romantic."

She laughed, and we had sex in one of the most romantic cities on Earth.

18

An Audience with the Pope

WHEN ALEJANDRA MENTIONED TO OUR kids' principal, Sister Colleen, that we were going to Rome in the summer, she told Alejandra that if the Pope was in Rome on a Wednesday, he did a Benediction for all the Pilgrims in St. Peter's Square at 9:30 a.m. "If Pope Francis is there," she said, "you are going to have to arrive at the Vatican early because they close the gates at 9 a.m."

As it turned out, Pope Francis was in town the same time we were in Rome, and therefore there was a Benediction. As practicing Catholics, we were going. It was our last day in Italy, and we'd hit all the sights in Rome prior to the Vatican: the Coliseum, the Forum, the Trevi Fountain, the Spanish Steps. Although I'm not going to diminish any of those incredible structures, how often do you see the Pope in person?

We woke up at 7 a.m. and took the subway to just outside the Vatican City. We had a three-block walk to the gates. We arrived at 8 a.m., and it was packed. We sat about fifteen rows from the barrier gates in the front, separating distinguished guests from the rest of the crowd. The Altar, which is in front of the Basilica, was a huge, twenty-by-twenty foot stage with a white canopy and one gold chair with red cushions on it, where the Pope sits.

Every seat was taken, and the security in St. Peter's Square was *very* present. From the Papal Guards dressed in their 1600 uniforms and the security men in black suits, white shirts, and black sunglasses, we knew that the Pope was well protected. We went through metal detectors just to get into the Square. Alejandra, who can make fast friends with anyone in ten seconds, met and befriended a couple from Chicago. They were talking, and the next thing I knew, they were giving us forty wooden string crosses from their brother, who was a carpenter. They told us, "During the Benediction, Pope Francis will bless anything you want blessed. All you have to do is hold it up."

"Nice," I said. We had twenty-five rosary beads and now forty wooden crosses to be blessed by the Pope.

While we were waiting and the square was filling up, angelic music played on the sound system. There were two, huge television screens on both sides of the Square about forty feet wide so that everyone could see the Pope. Taking all of this in under the hot sun of Rome, I broke down and started crying tears of joy. Alejandra saw me and cried as well, and we hugged each other, knowing this was an incredible moment in our lives. I'm not a perfect man at all, nor do I claim to be or think that I'm holier than thou, but I'll say this: if you can sit in St. Peter's Square, listen to the music, and not believe in God afterward, then something is wrong.

At 10 a.m., the Pope came among cheers and stood on top of the Pope mobile, waving to the crowd in his white gown and hat. The crowd erupted in thunderous applause as the popemobile made a pass of the entire crowd. The Pope got out of the mobile and ascended the steps of the Basilica to his chair on the stage.

The Benediction was spoken in several different languages (English, Spanish, French, German, Portuguese, and Italian). There was a priest for each language who recited the Benediction and then told Pope Francis of all the Pilgrims who came there today. A cheer went up from each language in the crowd.

Finally, it came time for Pope Francis to bless whatever you brought to be blessed, and I took out the rosary beads and crosses. Pope Francis gave us his blessing. When the Benediction ended, Pope Francis shook hands with the distinguished guests and chatted with them for a few moments. Some people left, but we stayed and took some incredible shots of the Pope close up. After an hour, Pope Francis entered the Basilica. We left St. Peter's Square because we had to, and we decided to get lunch at a nearby restaurant, because we were going to the Basilica and the Sistine Chapel at 12:30 p.m. when it reopened.

After lunch, we waited in an hour-long line to get into the Basilica. This was now my second time inside it, and it was still breathtaking. We looked all around the church and after an hour headed to the Sistine Chapel. On our way, we saw all the statues housed in the Basilica. Jack was especially excited to see a bust of Julius Caesar because he was studying him in school that past year. We took a photo.

We finally got into the Sistine Chapel, where there are no pictures allowed and mandated silence. Unfortunately, many people were not following this one rule, and an announcement in several languages in a loud voice echoed across the room, "Silence, please!" We took a seat on the wooden benches, and Allie sat next to me. Again the announcement went off. Allie whispered, "Daddy, is that Jesus?"

I started cracking up and quickly tried to stifle my laughter. "No, baby, that's a man trying to quiet everyone because it's too loud," I whispered back.

We left the Sistine Chapel and headed back to our Airbnb to shower and pack after a great trip. The most important thing we learned on this trip was that we could travel to Europe with our family, including the four-year-old, and have a fantastic time! In fact, we inspired a bunch of people who thought they would take that dream trip when their kids get older to book it now.

On her first day of school that fall, Allie didn't want to go. "Daddy, I want to go back to Italy! I miss my bed in Bologna!"

"I do, too, Allie. I do, too."

Epilogue

THIS STARTED OUT JUST "ALONG FOR THE RIDE," but the ride became an incredible adventure and life that Alejandra, our kids, and I have been living for the past fourteen years. I'm lucky to have experienced these amazing trips with her and look forward to many more of them in the future, God willing.